The Ethics of Paul Tillich

MERCER *Tillich* SERIES

MERCER UNIVERSITY

MERCER UNIVERSITY PRESS

Endowed by

TOM WATSON BROWN

and

THE WATSON-BROWN FOUNDATION, INC.

The Ethics of Paul Tillich

RONALD H. STONE

MERCER UNIVERSITY PRESS
Macon, Georgia
2021

MUP/ P634

Published by Mercer University Press
1501 Mercer University Drive
Macon, Georgia 31207

25 24 23 22 21 5 4 3 2 1

Books published by Mercer University Press are printed on acid-free paper that meets the requirements of the American National Standard for Information Sciences—Permanence of Paper for Printed Library Materials.

Printed and bound in the United States.

This book is set in Adobe Caslon Pro.

Cover/jacket design by Burt&Burt.

ISBN 978-0-88146-809-0.
Cataloging-in-Publication Data is available from the Library of Congress

Dedicated to

My Brothers,

Hugh Stone, Religious Scholar of Iowa

and

Roger Stone, Political Savant of the Prairie

CONTENTS

PREFACE

Paul Tillich exhibited an unusual amount of courage. This aspect of his character led me to write this book using essays I had published over forty years of scholarship on him and new chapters on his ethics and aspects of his thought and action that I had not previously explored. It is rather obvious that in our time Christians must find courage to think, write, and act with new vigor. It is hard for pastors and academics to act truthfully as their convictions tell them they should. Most of the churches are controlled by middle-class or upper-class men deeply committed to the practices of the American Empire. In the universities, action in popular culture or commitments to bold social action critical of the United States only seldom produce academic advancement or security. Too often pastors or professors are tamed by their constituents before they achieve full recognition in their profession. Then they tend to remain tamed, accepting the prevailing mores and policies of the United States.

Before he became a professor Tillich pastored workers in the Berlin suburbs and went to war for King, God, and Fatherland. Broken by the war he revolted against the status quo in a revolutionary situation demanding reform of church and nation. His radicalness continued and is still present in his last writings. His ethics are most clearly exposited in late life writings on ethics and in the final volume of *Systematic Theology*. This book follows his major social writings from the time of his exile from Hitler's Germany, but it will adopt as principles of interpretation of his ethics the perspective of these later writings. In *Morality and Beyond, Systematic Theology,* and *My Search for Absolutes* his conclusions about ethics are defined and summarized. In the years between these volumes his denunciations of the warmongering of Senator Goldwater and his unfitness for high office were no less bold than his earlier denunciation of Hitler which cost him his academic vocation and citizenship. In the Goldwater criticism, joined by Niebuhr, and Editor Wane Cowan, it only cost *Christianity and Crisis* its temporary tax exempt status.

Chapter 1

ETHICS AND MORALS

Morals are the rules, principles, commandments, narratives, and paradigms by which we decide what we ought to do when the question of right or good behavior arises. Ethics is the theory of morals for human behavior when the question of that which we ought to do develops. The ethics or theory of morals of Paul Tillich has been regarded as an ontological ethics, socialist ethics, situationalist ethics, and dialectical ethics. He is not always consistent, and an argument can be made for each of the above categories. My exploration of his writing on ethics leads me to regard his method as a principled-situationalist ethic. His ontology is a reoccurring part of his ethics. His writing a socialist ethic reveals his debts to socialist theory and practice. In places in the book the consistency between Tillich's actions or praxis and his ethical theory will be raised. He certainly emphasizes the "Situation" particularly in his late writings in the 1960s when situationalist ethics was prominent. As a dialectical theologian, he often refers to both a "Yes" and a "No" in answering questions.

Tillich's early life reflected the morals of his family, church, and university as that of most moralists. World War I and the following Bohemian culture of the Weimar Republic broke the conventional ethic. He suffered post-traumatic stress disorder from the fighting on the Western Front as he broke down. His wife's betrayal with his friend while he was at the war shook his conventional morality, and the church's failure to adjust to the new revolutionary situation alienated him from his spiritual heritage. He served the last months of the war in Berlin and he developed as a lecturer at the University of Berlin. His first lectures were on the church and contemporary society. He joined movements to reform the church and the society, but his own religious-socialist position was not accepted by either the church or the socialists.

He held on to the ethical absolute of Immanuel Kant, but the situation demanded a new morality. The absolute came to mean the obligation to act morally out of the human essence of the person as honoring the requirements of one's own nature. As a religious socialist much of his morality pointed in the teleological direction of the ends of the socialist society in a realization of the religious nature of humanity. For example, the provision of economic security for the masses was an oft repeated goal of his efforts. However, he considered the rights of humanity expressed as principles as immediately relevant to his social ethic and to the future society, so to this degree he was not a teleological thinker, but a deontological ethicist. One of his outstanding ethics texts, *Love, Power, and Justice*, is fundamentally ontological in nature as are many texts in the Harvard Archives of his speeches on ethics.[1] On many of the issues of war, he uses just war theory placing his work in a deontological or rule based ethic. Given the obvious complexities of Tillich's ethics, he is in one sense his own moral witness. At another dimension his ethical theory is synthetic, and we find different methods of ethical

[1] Roger L. Shinn, "Tension and Unity in the Ethics of Paul Tillich: An Exploration,' in *Being and Doing: Paul Tillich as Ethicist*, ed. John J. Carey (Macon: Mercer University Press, 1987), 9-28.

reflection in different historical epochs and situations. The unraveling of this complexity, particularly in terms of his later writings, is part of the task of this book.

There are only a few studies of his complete ethic.[2] Secondary literature on his philosophy of religion and theology is massive. The North American Paul Tillich Society keeps developing scholarship in both areas. This study is the first solo-authored book in English on his ethical theory. Recently some attention has been paid to his social thought, but his ethic is infrequently analyzed. This study includes chapters on social ethics from his developed philosophical perspective.

After World War I, Tillich's thought had to be reformulated. The helmet he wore proclaiming "For Fatherland with God and King" neither protected his brain from the blasts of artillery nor represented his thought by the end of the war. He continued the deep Frederick Schelling trajectories of his thought, but now he added Nietzsche, Kierkegaard, Marx and expressionist art in revolt against his youthful foundations of church, hierarchical family, and ordered German culture. Tillich's conscience, as a child and youth, was formed by patriarchal family, monarchy, and ordered German life, which betrayed him and his generation. That morality died in the trenches of the Western Front.

Immediately after the war he tried to reform the church in the direction of equal gender roles, commitment to peace, and social justice. But he failed. The bureaucratic critique of his efforts alienated him from the church. He saw the future as socialist and the church disestablished. He knew that the Enlightenment and the church's failures disinherited it from society. The society, he thought, was growing in a secular direction, and the church was losing its relevance. He set his mind loose to work as a theologian of

[2] John J. Carey, ed., *Being and Doing* is an impressive anthology of different perspectives on Tillich's ethic.

the culture rather than a church theologian.

He rejected the church's attempts to control society whether it was through Roman Catholic hierarchical power or Protestant Biblical interpretation. Modern society and particularly university faculties rebelled to overthrow the controlling hegemony of the Christian churches. The society was becoming autonomous, particularly in the new rebelling German society. The church could neither control nor persuade society in the old ways of theologically enforced morality.

However, the world depended upon the Unconditional and the sciences were truest when they recognized their mutual relationships and the presence of the Unconditional in their pursuit of truth and dependence upon order reflecting value. Therefore the role of the theologian of culture was to help the autonomous rebellious thought to find its roots in the Unconditional. Recognizing their autonomy from outdated church thought, the Unconditioned could still be relevant to their science. The task of the philosopher of religion was to discover and explain the theonomies (religious dimensions) within the various sciences. Ethics like aesthetics had its own place in the science of the universities, but it was autonomous from the church. Tillich's studies of law, ethics, the state, and economy located the humanistic realities of love in the sciences and professions. The mystical reality of love in the meaning of the sciences pointed toward the Unconditional. He saw truth in Kant, Hegel, and Schleiermacher. Schleiermacher's orientation toward the feeling of dependence was closest to the truth. But religion was more completely understood as: "Religion is not a feeling; it is an attitude of the spirit in which practical, theoretical, and emotional elements are united to form a complex whole."[3]

---

[3] Paul Tillich, "On the Idea of a Theology of Culture," in *What is Religion?*, ed. James Luther Adams, trans. William B. Green (New York: Harper & Row Publishers, 1969), 160.

THEOLOGIAN OF CULTURE

The theologian of culture seeks the theonomous ethics in the culture from his own free perspective while the church theologian explicates the ethics of a particular religious community. In the United States some theologians hold the two together while the distinction is understood. In his years in Germany hoping for socialism, Tillich's standpoint was as a theologian of culture, but in his attempts at systematic theology he held the two together. He held positions in philosophy and social philosophy. In the United States, Tillich as a philosopher of religion and systematic theologian would work in his writing as both a theonomous philosopher of culture and as a philosophical theologian with his ethics expressed both in theonomy of culture and theological ethics. The philosopher would be the freer, but the theologian would strive for a new theological vocabulary for the church. His writing on ethics in "The Idea of a Theology of Culture" does not disclose the particulars of morality or his affirmation of theonomous socialism as the future filled with the mysticism of love for which he hoped.

The philosopher influenced by his ethos from childhood can choose to affirm selective church tradition theonomously. In my *The Ultimate Imperative* as a philosopher-theologian I chose in my freedom selective aspects of the ethical tradition.[4] In my finite-freedom I chose love-justice, the Ten Commandments, an interpretation of Jesus' ethic, and a perspective from political philosophy. I argue other modern Christians should choose them as well. I would not choose Tillich's term of Unconditioned as a synonym for God, but I would choose Ultimate Concern as a concept. Contemporary philosophical theologians do not need to recognize all church tradition, hierarchical teaching, nor scripture as authoritative. But they are

[4] Ronald H. Stone, *The Ultimate Imperative* (Cleveland: The Pilgrim Press, 1990).

relevant for consideration and the choice will be determinative for a thinker. The first time I taught philosophical ethics at my alma mater I used ten different philosophers as sources to be read, and then the students in finite-freedom could choose the perspectives most convincing to them. As thinkers we do not build de novo; we choose from sources that we inherit whether from family or later from philosophy classes.

Tillich in the 1920s was alienated from church and state. The church hierarchy in Berlin silenced his public speaking on religious socialism. The church in Saxony opposed his appointment to a philosophy position in Dresden. Some in the church hierarchy were alienated by his Bohemian lifestyle and the new sexual freedom that replaced the earlier restricted life of the Wingolf Society of his student years. He was not a practicing member of a political party. He later admitted much of his thought in the 1920s was utopian. This is more obvious in "On the Idea of a Theology of Culture" than in *The System of the Sciences* (1933).[5] The place of ethics in the *System* remains idealist and the work of a philosopher of the Spirit. To cast ethics as the "science of the active realization of the Unconditional" is to remove it a long way from society. His statement that there is "only one duty and that is toward God," only picks up one fork of the Great Commandment. Tillich's idea that ethics is not to impinge upon law or community is more idealist than Tillich could be in reality. The later ethic of the 1960s, which regards it as the philosophy of human morals, reflects his evolution through *The Religious Situation* where ethics examines the youth revolt, the sexual revolution, and the praxis of education reflects his "belief-ful realism" or as I prefer "faithful realism" characteristic of his life. As an American building on *The Religious Situation*, the theology of culture absorbs much of the meaning of social ethics and so to grasp

[5] Paul Tillich, *The System of the Sciences According to Objects and Methods*, trans. Paul Wiebe (Lewisburg: Bucknell University Press, 1981), 198-203, 226.

the complexity of his thought moves beyond *The System of the Sciences*. This book examines his communities of socialism, praxis in World War, his struggle with anti-Semitism, the meaning of justice, love, and power, and his social commentary as the ethics he lived. However, continuity with the early *System* is reflected in the early system's conclusion: that love is found in justice. In this early stage ecclesiastical ethics receives little attention as he is moving ahead to a society grounded in socialism which will produce a meaningful society focused on the Unconditional orientation of academic disciplines. The state, community and law will bear the meaning of ideal groups such as sectarians understood themselves as church within the church. For the theology of culture the old categories of social ethics, personal ethics or theological ethics lose their purpose as society is examined by a theonomous philosophy of culture. In reality both Communists and Fascists attempted to change reality, so the controllers of the state expressed their meanings and socialist meaning was crushed for years.

In his recognition of the preservation of the theological faculties in German universities Tillich returned to his realism, but he hoped they would produce theologies of culture. Later in America, his institution of Union Theological Seminary appointed him both as a philosopher of religion and professor of theology. Christian ethics claimed its own department in the theological field, but its professors also taught theology. Moreover the professors of theology, Daniel Williams, Ian Macquarrie, and Paul Lehman, also wrote books on ethics as did Tillich. My own experience there was to assist in teaching theology before I taught ethics.

MATURE ETHICS

Tillich's ethics was submerged when he was writing as a socialist philosopher thinking he was living in a revolutionary time. The religious vision of socialism bases so much on the transformation of the system that it does not adjust its focus sufficiently to the present living in less than a transformed situation. His mature ethics are in *Systematic Theology*, vol. 3, *Morality and Beyond*, and *My Search for Absolutes.* His study of theological ethics in a book on morality was published in 1963 as he was publishing *Systematic Theology.* The posthumously published volume on absolutes in 1967 finished his work on ethics. Ruth Nanda Ashen, the editor, credited Hannah Tillich and Robert Kimball as advising in the last publication. It is safe to take the essay "The Absolute and the Relative Element in Moral Decision" as a definitive source for his mature theory of morality as informed by his autobiographical essay in the same book. The three chapters of the book were lectures at the University of Chicago Law School and he intended them for a later presentation of the Noble Lectures at Harvard University.

The absolute of the moral imperative was most clearly presented by Immanuel Kant. Tillich follows Kant in recognizing the autonomy of the moral imperative arising from the essence of personhood which cannot be violated. If we recognize an imperative as moral, we are obligated to follow it categorically or to risk destroying the meaning of our morality. For Tillich a violation of the moral imperative would deny our dignity as a person. He notes that religious ethics may regard the imperatives as the will of God. For Tillich such symbolic language is another way of meaning the imperative is of true essence. Of course, in fact, obedience to the imperative is another matter. If situations are very concrete, no code of morality can be particular as to time, place, context, and consequence. Normally one can live within the expectation of one's society, but such mores are relative to the culture. No moral code is ever safe from particulars and interpretation. Even the norm "do no harm" requires interpretation in the doctor's responsibility to speak the truth, but to protect the patient's health. Conscience is also not a sure guide. No outside guide can determine morality for unique situations. The person must often risk a choice. Cultural changes and revolutions also change norms; witness twenty-first century changes in sexual mores and women's roles in Western society.

In a dynamic, pluralistic society hard decisions keep coming at a person. Some will retreat into traditional patterns. Others who have abandoned the traditional answers face new decisions about religion, vocation, sexuality, and politics. These have to face moral decisions in face of the absolute demand of love and relative principles of morality including justice. Justice means different guidance in different moral systems and times. For Tillich justice means "Creative justice" and in Christian theology it is grounded in *agape* which means overcoming relativism and seeking reunion with the other and God.

Love includes justice. Society lacks the deciding, personal-centered action, and justice is the more significant principle there. If Tillich is referring to social forces, justice may be the highest relevant principle. I have found both Jewish rabbis and Arab sheiks insisting justice is the highest principle of morality in our dialogues. Tillich's meaning of *agape* includes "Listening love," which looks at the concrete situation and the motives of others. The situation is helpfully explored by knowledge gained through psychology, sociology, and economics. In the latter pages Tillich published, he could be regarded as a situationalist ethicist. John Carey, a preeminent scholar of Tillich's ethics, so regarded him. Personally, I believe further study of his late ethics and the chapter in *My Search for Absolutes* carry him beyond the situationalist position in ethics.

Tillich goes beyond the highest principle of *agape* and the loving study of the situation to the wisdom of moral principles and science. Here the principles of the Ten Commandments, The Sermon on the Mount, or the moral traditions of other religions are to be utilized. It is dangerous to override the moral traditions in one's autonomy. The moral traditions of humanity are drawn from human experience and are valuable. The wisdom of the ages is not easily overturned. I think the Ten Commandments may be accepted in freedom and they are less burdensome and more subject to free-responsible interpretation than Tillich granted. Tillich's "Grand Inquisitor" lurked in his ethics as Karl Barth suggested. He was the son of a German-Prussian, a District Superintendent of pastors, repressed at home and by his Wingolf Society, he had much to overcome. As a youth, he had to meet standards more severe than his fellow liberally educated American professors ever faced or feared. However far they may move, writers on ethics have as their first teachers their parents, and then they modify their ethics as they learn philosophy and other disciplines.

That which Tillich relativized in criticizing moral codes, he brought back as moral wisdom to be used in free-moral decision making. America, relatively grounded in competition, needs these principles of moral wisdom to save itself. Tillich concluded his formal writing on morality in the hope that one would neither flee in normlessness nor seek false security in dead tradition. The interpretation of this book chooses to interpret his ethics in his threefold pattern of free moral choice: (1) The interpretation of *agape* including justice as the absolute moral imperative; (2) The recognition of moral principles as relative moral wisdom to be applied in moral judgments; (3) The need for "loving listening" to the situation including its analysis through the relevant human sciences. In the interpretation of all of his writings on morality are discovered elements of ontology, paradox, situationalism, and moral traditions of philosophy and religious tradition, but the dominant path is found in the threefold analysis of moral choice, risking mistakes and trusting that the absolute of *agape* accepts mistakes in forgiveness and loves the moral order.

Chapter 2

CONVERSATIONS IN RELIGIOUS SOCIALIST CIRCLES[1]

From 1975-1990, I wrestled with Paul Tillich's commitment to religious socialism. This search to understand why a realist would commit himself to a utopian cause occupied my mind in many diverse ways. Beyond Tillich, I was attracted to the revolutionary possibilities for Latin America of religious socialism in the movement of liberation theology. It, too, failed. My own movement has taken me to a Christian-democratic, mixed-economy version of what could be a religiously influenced, fair America. The conclusion is not that different from Tillich's, except he did not ever surrender the vision of a religious socialism.

This process of inquiry into the roots of Tillich's religious socialist commitments revealed that these were communal projects. His insights, conclusions, and decisions were formed in conversation

---

[1] This chapter was previously published in Mary Ann Stenger and Ronald H. Stone, *Dialogues of Paul Tillich* (Macon: Mercer University Press, 2002), 164-87.

with others who were struggling to articulate a vision of reform for their societies. He was never without these partners in conversation, and the specific economic dimensions of his hopes were particularly dependent upon experienced economists. He would often lead in the philosophy of history and religious conceptual discussions while others like Eduard Heimann or Reinhold Niebuhr would lead in the economic or political dimensions of the discussion. The discussions were from 1918-1955, but three specific groups can be isolated as the most important for his search: The Kairos Circle, The Frankfurt School, and The Fellowship of Socialist Christians.

KAIROS CIRCLE

The Kairos Circle, also known as "the Berlin Circle," the "circle around Tillich and Mennicke," or "the circle around the *Blätter für religiösen Sozialismus,*" met every week or two in a restaurant or a home for discussion. It had evolved under Carl Mennicke, Günther Dehn, and Paul Tillich's leadership as they had moved out of the *Soziale Arbeitsgemeinschaft.* Günther Dehn, a member until about 1923, wrote that it never grew to more than ten or twelve members. Various commentators list different participants. Eberhard Amelung's list,[2] combined with the list from John Stumme,[3] produces the following names: Günther Dehn, Eduard Heimann, Adolf Löewe, William Löwe, Hans Hartmann, Carl Mennicke, Trude Mennicke, Gustav Radbruch, August Rathmann, Hugo Sinzheimer, Karl Ludwig Schmidt, Hans Simmons, Paul Tillich, and Arnold Wolfers, giving a maximum number of fourteen.[4] The group functioned for Tillich from 1920 until 1924, when he moved to Marburg. Some

---

[7] Eberhard Amelung, "Religious Socialism as an Ideology: A Study of the Kairos Circle in Germany between 1919-1933" (doctoral dissertation, Harvard University, 1962), microfilm.

[8] John R. Stumme, *Socialism in Theological Perspective: A Study of Paul Tillich, 1918-1933* (Missoula: Scholars Press, 1978), 35.

[4] Stumme, 62.

members assembled several times later and kept in touch by correspondence, conferences, etc. For Tillich the Kairos Circle, as it originally functioned, concluded with his departure from Berlin. The ideas developed there continued to appear in his thought. Carl Mennicke and Adolf Löwe shared his company and influenced his thought through Frankfurt. In New York he reunited with Eduard Heimann and Adolf Löwe. Mennicke survived the war in concentration camps.

My reading of the Kairos Circle supports the conclusion of Stumme's critique of Amelung. The circle was not dominated totally by Tillich's ideas; most of these were not intellectuals to be dominated. The circle did not have the same ideas, but they shared some of the same problems upon which they reflected. The circle was as broad as Christian and atheist, socialist and communist. The journal of the circle attained about 500 in circulation and was published from 1920-1927. The group had only minimal commitments to either church or party; an alienation out of which Tillich could conjure up the virtue of finding a new way. They maintained some contact with other religious socialist groups but did not merge with them.

Mennicke summarized the group's conversations as having four major roles: (1) Barth's theology, (2) Marxism, (3) proletariat, and (4) the shape of the future socialist society.[5] But they were united in their conversations as much by the heady political climate and pressures of their day as they were by ideology.

The foundations of the world order seemed to be shaking. The death throes of the old empire prevented the emergence of a new order, and the forces for the new order were divided among bourgeois, fascist, and radical groups. The political issue explicated in the concept of Tillich's Kairos group was: How can we affirm action for decisive change without surrendering to the enthusiasms of the activists? Or, how can we mediate between the determinists and the

[5] Stumme, 34.

romantic activists? Experience taught that action or praxis was vital to social change, but action had to be in accord with the objective social conditions. In religious terms the question around the Kairos Circle was: How does the eternal relate to the temporal? To combine the religious and the political question meant to ask: When are moments of historical action eternally significant?

The essay "Kairos" is a call to a consciousness of history that is grounded in the "depth of the Unconditional."[6] The Unconditional is expressed as a quality of experience which is absolute or ultimate. It is captured in the first commandment, "Thou shalt love the Lord thy God with all thy heart." It is a philosophy of history set against all forms of understanding history that deny it meaning.

The concept of *kairos* has its origins in the New Testament as "right time" rather than chronos or "formal time." The demands and opportunities of each time vary. The moments of absolute demand are the moments of *kairos*.[7] The idea that particular times are filled with significance is contrasted both to Eastern mystical tendencies which would deny the significance of history and to Western mechanistic thinking which would obscure the significance of history.

The danger of the crisis theology of Karl Barth was that the significance of the present might be eclipsed. Barth was correct to relativize all historical creations. There is no absolute church or absolute state. But Tillich insists when an old order is passing and a new order is emerging, the new order is *en kairos*. The new order is subject to judgment and change, but its coming is the content of history. For Tillich, obviously, the new socialist order was in the right time in the early Weimar Republic.

The philosophy of history represented by *kairos* is a form of dialectical interpretation of history. There is no final stage in the *kairos* interpretation. The stage of the spirit of Joachim of Flora or the

---

[6] Paul Tillich, "Kairos," in *The Protestant Era* (Chicago: The University of Chicago Press, 1948), 32.

[7] Tillich, 33.

classless society of Marx is not to be thought of as final stages; they, too, are subject to criticism and transformation. The concept of *kairos* tries to retain the idea of classical history that each moment is significant and also the progressive conviction of progress in the appearance of the new in history. The dialectical interpretation united the above two, and the addition of the *kairos* doctrine amended the dialectical interpretation.

Tillich settles for a paradox. In the moment of *kairos* the absolute is expressed, but yet it is not an absolute. Judgment and further transformation await every realization. The proper response in such a situation is to refrain from trying to capture the absolute; rather, one should surrender to it. Christ, as the one who surrenders the self, is clearly the norm for life in moments of *kairos*. As Christ reveals the individual surrendering to the universal, so in moments of personal *kairos* or social *kairos* the particular is to be surrendered to the universal. Clearly, Tillich is using his Christology as a formulation for philosophy of history, but for him the secular images of "the third epoch of world history" or the "Kingdom of God" can express the same reality.[8]

A time of *kairos* was confronting the Western world. Religious socialism was the theological interpretation of socialism in light of the *kairos* philosophy. Here in 1922 the rudimentary ideas that were to be expressed in *The Religious Situation* of 1926 and *The Socialist Decision* of 1932 are present. The task of religious socialism was the theoretical task of reminding socialism of its roots in the Unconditional. Religious socialism had to attempt to free socialism from its bourgeois loyalties. Tillich rejected the attempts to unite socialism with the churches, for the alliance would only strengthen them, whereas both needed to be thoroughly criticized and transformed.

In 1951 he returned to Berlin and lectured at the *Deutsche Hochschule für Politik* with which many of the original members of

[8] Tillich, 43.

the Kairos Circle had been associated. His lectures were on Utopia, but he returned to the doctrine of the *kairos*. He expressed the concept of *kairos* as a way of saying both yes and no at the moment of decision. Yes could be said to the demand for absolute action. However, no was said to the demand for idolatry. New orders can be born in history; but they, too, will be transformed. Fulfillment, he said, is found in the vertical dimension of history; on the horizontal level fulfillment is always fragmentary.[9] Looking back on history since the end of World War I, he concluded that the interwar reflections on *kairos* were correct.

The final part of *Systematic Theology* returned to the theme of *kairos* and acknowledged the emergence of the term in the context of religious socialism.[10] In part the *kairos* which was expected had been fulfilled, in part it had not arrived, and in part it was betrayed by the Nazis. "Awareness of a kairos is a matter of vision."[11] It is the surrendering to the spirit which is doing something new. It is a full affirmation of what is happening beyond calculation and analysis. Such affirmation is, of course, subject to error. Against theologians or philosophers who supported the Nazis, Tillich argued the "Cross of the Christ was and is the absolute criterion."[12] Moments of *kairos* are rare, and, as for Tillich himself, he regarded the interwar period as a time of *kairos* and thought that a future *kairos* for Western civilization was postponed until the rather distant future.

RELIGIOUS SOCIALISM

In 1923 Tillich published in the journal of the Kairos Circle, *Blätter für religiösen Sozialismus,* a lengthy essay, "Basic Principles of

[9] Paul Tillich, *Political Expectation*, ed. James Luther Adams (New York: Harper & Row Publishers, 1971), 179.

[10] Paul Tillich, *Systematic Theology*, vol. 3 (Chicago: The University of Chicago Press, 1963), 369-72.

[11] Tillich, 370.

[12] Tillich, 371.

Religious Socialism."[13] The essay incorporates work from *The System of the Sciences,* published in the same year, which he had been working on since his days on the Western Front. Some of the concepts of the essay are also found in a more developed form in his "Philosophy of Religion" published in 1925. The work also suggests ideas which are more fully developed in his 1933 *The Socialist Decision.*

Religious socialism as a movement is identified with neither a church nor a political party. It is a community of those who are grasped by the *kairos* of a new time and who are hoping that the emerging order can be religious and socialist. It joins in the socialist political struggles, but it does not want to bless them with religious sanction. The tactics of the socialist parties do not express the fullness of the socialist idea.[14]

Religious socialism, according to Tillich, is an attempt to reunite the sacramental basis of society with historical critical consciousness. In religion such a union would be represented by a synthesis of Catholic substance and Protestant critique. In society, the union is a meaningful society utilizing modern technique.

The goal of religious socialism is nothing less than theonomy. Theonomy means the sovereignty of God or "God is all in all." He distinguishes theonomy from both other-worldly utopianism and this-worldly utopianism.[15] It preserves the "yes" of religion to socialism as well as the religious reservation of religion to socialism. Similarly, the religion which negates itself is most open to what the spirit is doing in society. Expressed in terms of social ethics, theonomy is the right and the just. Concretely, it is seen in its opposition to demonic distortions of humanity's life.

In the area of economy, Tillich argues that the modern, rational economy denies personality as fully as did the ancient order. He

---

[13] Paul Tillich, "Basic Principles of Religious Socialism" in *Political Expectation* (New York: Harper & Row Publishers, 1971), 58-88.

[14] Tillich, 88.

[15] Tillich, 62.

looks for a restoration of an eros relationship between person and thing. The meaning is not clear, but it seems that his intention was not that different from the young Marx, the overcoming of the person's alienation from product. There is explicit rejection of the criticism of machines; rather the need is to find a new scheme of meaning that will allow people to participate meaningfully in a "mythos of technology."[16] The pattern is a familiar one for Tillich, the critique of modern autonomous society, and the seeking of a new basis for it.

The rational, capitalist society is organized demonically in that its foundation is the war of all against all in competition. The class struggle reveals the disharmony underlying the capitalist order. The reduction of all relationships of power and eros to economic terms denies the individual his subjective rights and leaves only objective dependent relationships. In the new society envisaged by Tillich, there is a return to some models associated with feudal society; but, of course, without inherited wealth or privileged families without responsibilities for community functions. He mentions the idea of "fief," whereby one has disposition of goods in relationship to the needs of the community. The society has a certain hierarchy of function as determined by those of the whole. Ideas of property through fief and representative property replace both state ownership and private ownership in his understanding of religious socialism.[17]

At the present time, the state is the defender of justice. Justice is upheld by power. Religious socialism rejects various forms of anarchism and accepts the present reality of the state while combating nationalism, particularly in its idolatrous forms. As Tillich hopes for an aristocracy to emerge that will represent the struggle for a theonomous society, so in international affairs he hopes "the strongest bearers of the theonomous idea of humanity should constitute the

[16] Tillich, 76.
[17] Tillich, 79.

leadership of nations."[18] There is a religious reservation about force. Tolstoy symbolizes such a reservation, but religious socialism cannot abandon the power that will sustain justice. The particular expressions of the theonomous society were for Tillich provisional. Meanwhile, religious socialists were to struggle to overthrow the demonic in education, state, and culture while awaiting the breakthrough to the new society.[19]

Tillich's writing on religious socialism in the turmoil of Berlin expressed the spirit of utopianism more than it did faithful realism. His awareness of the class struggle kept him from endorsing the SPD, but he could not give himself enthusiastically to the Independents either. The idea of *kairos* would remain central to this philosophy of society, but later reflection on the class struggle and a continuing discussion with social philosophers would in Dresden and Frankfurt produce a more realistic political outlook. From Frankfurt in 1930, he reflected on those earlier years of excitement in Berlin:

> That was the spiritual situation in the five years after the Revolution, full of passion and power, full of despair and consciousness of death, full of the mood of doom and yearning. We still feel it in our blood, but we also know that something different has come into existence since then. All who had been broken and not built anew in those years experience a remarkable surprise; under closer examination that which they had created anew often very much resembled that which they had destroyed. The power of the old proved stronger than the five years of crisis had foreshadowed. Everywhere a reaction set in.[20]

Socialism had both universal and particular aspects. Its particular aspect depended on its being borne by the historical movement of the proletariat. To the extent that the Kairos Circle connected socialism and the proletariat, it risked its analysis upon the

---

[18] Tillich, 82.

[19] Tillich, 88.

[20] Paul Tillich, "Die Geisteslage der Gegenwart," in *Gesammelte Werke*, 10 (Stuttgart: Evangelisches Verlagswerk, 1926), 116.

consciousness of the proletariat. Heimann had seen the danger:

> If labor would cease to be socialistic, if it would agree to be accepted in socialism due to some socio-political and some bourgeois concessions, then it would no longer make sense to be a socialist; we intellectual socialists of bourgeois descent would then be unmasked as ideologists and romanticists; we would be like fish in a stream that is dried up.[21]

THE SOCIAL CONTEXT OF THE FRANKFURT SCHOOL

As Professor of Philosophy and Sociology at the University of Frankfurt (1929-33), Paul Tillich was closely associated with the membership of the *Institut für Sozialforschung* from the time of his arrival in Frankfurt. According to Horst Bögeholz, his appointment to the university was opposed by some of the philosophers. By the time of his expulsion in 1933, he was Dean of the Faculty. The *Institut* was dedicated to social research and the development of a critical theory of society. The membership of the *Institut* was left Hegelian or humanist-Marxist in inspiration and left of the Social Democrats of the Weimar Republic in politics.

Tillich's relationship to the *Institut für Sozialforschung* is important to an understanding of his social philosophy. His support and encouragement of the critical theory of *the Institut für Sozialforschung* indicates the type of social theory and research that interested him. Furthermore, Tillich's social theory had been a social product since Berlin. He worked his ideas out in discussion, and he wrote in loyalty to those with whom he talked. He brought Adolph Löwe and Eduard Heimann from Berlin into the intimate discussion group he shared with members of the *Institut*. His help to Horkheimmer in acquiring the chairmanship of the *Institut* shifted the *Institut* from Marxist economics to a much broader social critique.

---

[21] Eduard Heimann, *Kapitalismus und Sozialismus* (Potsdam: Alfred Protte, 1931), 189. Translated by author.

The *Institut's* wrestling with the theory-praxis question and the *Institut's* conclusion of seeking truth in theory characterized Tillich's struggles. His own relative withdrawal from *praxis* to write his *Systematic Theology* was a decision understandable in light of the *Institut's* social reality. The movement from Marxist social philosophy to Freudian psychoanalysis was a movement not of a solitary Tillich, but of a social group seeking a synthesis. Tillich's characteristic ways of addressing the issues of utopian thought, anti-Semitism, and economic theory were molded by his discussions with the members of the *Institut* and their associates. Reflection upon the social reality of the *Institut* is one avenue for understanding the Germanic origins of this immigrant's philosophy of culture and religion and its impact upon North America.

Tillich was close friends of three leaders of the *Institut*: Max Horkheimer, director from 1929; Leo Lowenthal; and Friedrich Pollock. Together with Karl Mannheim, Kurt Riezler, Adolph Löwe, and Karl Mennicke, the above formed a Kränzchen, or intimate discussion group.[22] The group, which was of importance to Tillich's thought, was often hosted by him first in Frankfurt and later in exile in New York City.

The *Institut* was independently endowed, though it cooperated with the University of Frankfurt. The independence of the *Institut* from state, university, and private capital enabled it to proceed in its own fashion to develop its critical theory. Those attracted to the *Institut* after 1929 were in large measure Marxists who could support neither the Communist line as practiced in Russia nor the socialism of the Weimar Republic in its diluted trade unionist and practical

---

[22] Martin Jay, *The Dialectical Imagination: A History of the Frankfurt School and the Institute of Social Research, 1923-1950* (Boston: Little, Brown and Company, 1973), 24.

political form.[23] Rather they undertook to reform the intellectual roots of Marxism and sought their inspiration in empirical research, cultural criticism, and the philosophy of the young Marx.

Independence from outside contact was, on the other hand, alienation from responsibility for society. Tillich was more involved in active socialist politics than were most members of the *Institut*. Most members were distant from the push and shove of responsible politics. They were closer to Max Weber's "ethic of absolute ends" than to the ethic of responsibility. However, they understood themselves as critical scholars of politics, not as politicians.[24]

Tillich was at the height of his German academic career as Professor of Philosophy in Frankfurt. At forty-three years of age his influence was widely felt, and he and Hannah Tillich lived a brilliant and exciting life in Frankfurt.[25] Part of this life was the frequent dinners and parties and the continuous discussion around the social situation with Karl Mannheim, Erich Fromm, Herbert Marcuse, and Max Horkheimer joining the debate. After 1930 the shadows began to deepen, and cultural expressions turned more to nihilism. Aryan-Semitic disputes began to fracture the University. The Tillichs' friendships were largely among the Jewish intellectual circles.[26] Hannah relates that he was in jest referred to as "Paulus among the Jews." Their families and friends came to divide among those supporting the Nazis and those allied with either the communists or the socialists. While attending a Nazi rally, Tillich perceived the demonic in Hitler. Then he began his critique of politics, *The Socialist Decision*, which was published in January 1933 and then suppressed.

---

[23] Peter Gay, "Weimar Culture: The Outsider as Insider," in *Perspectives in American History*, vol. 2 (Cambridge: Charles Warren Center for Studies in American History, 1968), 36.

[24] Gay, 36.

[25] Hannah Tillich, "Frankfurt," in *From Time to Time* (New York: Stein and Day, 1973) 141-56.

[26] Hannah Tillich, 149.

With the political deterioration of 1932, panic ensued among the Frankfurt circle. The endowment of the *Institut* had been established abroad in 1931 to provide for its possible continuation in exile. The pace of life became faster as if all of life had to be lived before the end. Paul Tillich was among the first university professors to be dismissed in 1933 by the Nazi regime. Of the twelve dismissed at Frankfurt, one was Tillich, and the other eleven were Jewish. He considered the underground; friends advised him against it. Max Horkheimer feared that Tillich's hopes for a change in the German situation would cause him to linger too long and result in his death. In fact, in February 1933, he read Tillich a line from one of his writings and told him that "if he would not leave Germany, it would cost him his life."[27] Tillich toured the country pondering his decision. In Dresden he missed arrest by the Gestapo only by a friend's forewarning.

They prepared to leave Germany, but still Tillich hesitated. Finally, realizing that no academic appointment was possible without recantation of his work, he had a final interview with the Nazi secretary of education. The secretary's responses to Tillich's queries about the Jews and modern culture were unsatisfying. The secretary suggested Tillich leave Germany.[28] The decision was made.

Tillich's years at Frankfurt came to an end as an act of political power. The power which dismissed him was the power he had analyzed and resisted. Friends in New York, particularly Horace Friess of Columbia University and Reinhold Niebuhr of Union Theological Seminary, had seen the danger, and upon his dismissal from Frankfurt secured him an academic appointment at Union. Horace Friess met the Tillichs when their ship docked. Ursula Niebuhr helped them settle into their first apartment in Knox Hall, part of

---

[27] Max Horkheimer, "Erinnerungen An Paul Tillich," in *Werk und Wirken Paul Tillich* (Stuttgart: Evangelisches Verlagswerk, 1967), 17. Translated by author.

[28] Hannah Tillich, *From Time*, 155.

the Union Seminary quadrangle on 122nd Street near the corner of Broadway. Soon the *Institut für Sozialforschung* was to join them in exile in its new home at Columbia University just across Broadway.

Tillich made many contributions to the *Institut*. He helped found a chair of social philosophy for Max Horkheimer to fill when he assumed the directorship.[29] He assisted Theodore Adorno in securing his first position at Frankfurt. He shared with Mannheim, Horkheimer, and Sinzheimer the dismissal from the university on April 13, 1933. He urged the *Institut's* reestablishment in Frankfurt in June 1949, hoping to renew social research and modern social science in Germany.[30]

The *Institut*, through its research, publication, and conversation, created a model of social reality which is reflected in several areas of Tillich's thought. The model reflected the personalities and minds of the members of the *Institut*. The model can be seen in: (1) the critical distance of philosophy from practical politics; (2) the combination of Freud and Marx; (3) the problem of utopian reflection; and (4) the economic theory.

In intellectual heritage and sociological position at Frankfurt, Tillich shared the position of the leading members of the *Institut*. This location in the broad spectrum of Left Hegelian young Marxist thought, and the academic elite of Frankfurt, kept most of them from active commitment to political parties. In the thirties the proletariat was not behaving according to Marxist philosophy, and the wrath of the petit bourgeoisie was about to make the location of the *Institut* in Germany impossible. They were the alienated intellectuals. Tillich would vote socialist, and in 1929 he joined the Social Democratic Party, but the compromises of the socialist party kept him from enthusiastically endorsing it. The communist awkwardness kept him out of their circles. When he published his major work

---

[29] Horkheimer, "Erinnerungen An Paul Tillich," 16.

[30] Jay, *Dialectical Imagination*, summary.

in politics, *The Socialist Decision*, it called for sophisticated reforms in socialism which the socialist leaders were intellectually and sociologically incapable of making. Its economics reflected the thought of Löwe more than it did the earlier Marxism of the *Institut*.

Critical theory as represented by Horkheimer, Adorno, and Marcuse, was suspicious of finished political-philosophical systems. The work of the school was in large part a critique of the intellectual tradition. Tillich shared the suspicion of existing systems, but he labored to produce a new synthesis. These synthetic attempts in Germany were largely unnoticed. His *System of the Sciences* received very few reviews. *The Socialist Decision* was consumed by the Nazi holocaust. His first volume of *Systematic Theology*, announced for 1927, did not appear until after his death. The American *Systematic Theology* of three volumes started appearing in 1951, and it lacked the thorough analysis of religious symbol and political philosophy which had been promised in the announcement for the 1927 volume. Fromm and Marcuse were to contribute their works of synthesis in the United States in their unification of Freudian and Marxian perspectives. Tillich's work in the United States was to incorporate the Freudian perspective more and more into his theological synthesis, while playing down the Marxian elements; but with the gradual discrediting in his mind of Neo-Marxist philosophy, his final synthetic works of philosophical theology were not to have a totally integrated political philosophy. The critical transcendence that characterized the Frankfurt school's politics while Tillich was there, from 1929-1933, was finally dominant in his major work.

Tillich's closest friends in the *Institut*, Adorno, Horkheimer, and Marcuse, were all involved in psychoanalysis and/or the relationship of sociological theory to Freudian theory. In the early 1930's it was intellectually radical, almost academically taboo, to relate Marxism and Freudianism. Neither Communism nor the psychoanalytic movement would touch the synthesis. Nevertheless, the *Institut* went ahead, merging Freud and Marx. Some problems with

Marxism seemed insolvable without new resources. Horkheimer received appreciative letters from Freud for his work in getting the Frankfurt Psychoanalytic Institute tied to the University of Frankfurt.[31]

Erich Fromm gradually moved from his synthetic work at the *Institut* to reject crucial components of Freud's theory, including aspects of the concept of libido.[32] Marx came to play a much larger role in his thought. He opted for Marx's view of possible human reconciliation and gradually shook off Freudian pessimism. As a result, he was dismissed by the International Psychoanalytic Association and regarded as a revisionist.

Adorno, Fromm, Horkheimer, and Marcuse's differences about Freud did not become apparent until emigration. In America, Horkheimer attacked Fromm's revisionist form of Freudianism. He argued that Freud's sociological setting in bourgeois Vienna was not necessarily detrimental to the theory. Freud was correct that psychology was intended to focus on the individual, not society. The libido was a necessary concept. Reconciliation could not precede social reconstruction. Theory could not be complete until social contradictions were resolved.[33]

Marcuse's use of Freud to correct Marx followed his disappointment over the purges of Stalin and the cruelties of the Spanish Civil War.[34] In *Eros and Civilization*,[35] he presented Freud as a revolutionary utopian. Fromm's critique was thoroughgoing. The debate between the two ranged over issues of exegesis of Freud, the character of civilization, the possibility of integrated personalities, the nature of love, and the meaning of tolerance. The issues of the *Institut* of the thirties were to continue to boil over into the United

---

[31] Jay, 88.

[32] Jay, 90.

[33] Jay, 102-3.

[34] Jay, 107.

[35] Herbert Marcuse, *Eros and Civilization* (Boston: Beacon Press, 1955).

States of the 1960s and '70s.

Terry Cooper wrote the book that was needed to explore Tillich's psychological theoretical work in the United States.[36] He was interested in the New York Psychological group and only mentioned the work of the Institute in Frankfurt. This chapter does not attempt to analyze his psychoanalytic theory but only argues that the move from Marx toward Freud was a move within a community of scholars. It was not simply a retreat from politics, but a way of becoming more "critical" of politics. It should also be noted that Tillich, like most other intellectuals, would respond to an invitation to lecture on a subject that was within his range of interest and competence. The fact that he used more Freudian terminology and lectured on psychology is in large part due to American disinterest in Marxian terminology and social revolution. Herbert Marcuse, in his preface to *Eros and Civilization*, indicated his indebtedness to Max Horkheimer and the *Institut* for his theoretical position and began: here psychological terms are now seen as political categories. This insight

[36] Terry Cooper, *Paul Tillich and Psychology* (Macon: Mercer University Press, 2006). Guyton B. Hammond has contributed a very valuable volume, *Man in Estrangement: A Comparison of the Thought of Paul Tillich and Erich Fromm* (Nashville: Vanderbilt University Press, 1965). His later work has contributed to understanding the intricacies of Tillich's relationship to critical theory as formulated in the *Institut*. See Guyton B. Hammond, "Tillich and the Frankfurt Debates about Patriarchy and the Family," in *Theonomy and Autonomy*, ed. John J. Carey (Macon: Mercer University Press, 1984) 89-110; Guyton B. Hammond, "Tillich and the Frankfurt School on Protestantism and the Bourgeois Spirit," in *Religion et Culture*, eds. Michel Despland, Jean-Claude Petit, and Jean Richard (Quebec, Les Presses de L'universite Laval, 1987) 327-38; Guyton B. Hammond, "Why Did Westerners Become Fascists? Fromm, Tillich, and Horkheimer on Character Types," *Papers from the Annual Meeting of the North American Paul Tillich Society* (September 1990): 8-12; Guyton B. Hammond, "Paul Tillich and the Frankfurt School," in *Applied Christianity*, ed. Matthew Lon Weaver (London: Lexington Books, 2014), 21-34. See Paul Tillich, *The Meaning of Health*, ed. Perry LeFevre (Chicago: Exploration Press, 1984).

of the *Institut* was shared in Tillich's thought.

Fromm's thought contained progressive utopian elements which distinguished his work from the critical, negative character of the work of the *Institut*. Others associated with the *Institut*, especially Benjamin, Horkheimer, and Adorno, used their utopian visions as principles of critique of the present, not as plans for the future. There was a deep note of pessimism in their work, which Tillich shared.

Utopian hopes kept history moving and negated the need for a mythological glorification of the present. Utopia, related to the prophetic spirit, confronted the "is" with an "ought." Tillich died in 1965, so we do not know his reaction to the Neo-Marxist activism of the late 1960s. However, he had opposed similar activism in the 1930s because he was looking for a middle way. Adorno expressed his dismay that much of the ideological fervor of the activists came from the theoretical work of the *Institut*. Martin Jay argued that Adorno's regrets pointed to "a fundamental conclusion of the theory itself: negation could never be truly negated."[37] With the dissolution of the proletariat, utopia had only a critical function.

For Tillich, finally, "it is the spirit of utopia that conquers utopia."[38] This means that utopia is distinguished from the Kingdom of God. It contains the idea that there are particularly significant times in history in which much can be accomplished. It also and most forcefully means that the freedom of the human spirit is such that no form of human organization will fulfill it. The human spirit is truly led to strive beyond its present boundaries, but while the Kingdom of God may be realized momentarily in human history as the vertical dimension intersects the horizontal dimension, fulfillment is never complete. Life continues as a tragic-ironic existence in

---

[37] Jay, *Dialectical Imagination*, 279.

[38] Paul Tillich, "The Political Meaning of Utopia," in *Political Expectations*, ed. James Luther Adams (New York: Harper & Row Publishers, 1971), 180.

which the critical function must be practiced.

Quite clearly, Tillich's theological affirmations were not shared by the secular Jews who dominated the *Institut*. Some of the members moved more toward religious affirmations in later life. Paul Tillich's influence on Eduard Heimann, leading even to his eventual baptism, is a particular case in point. Terence O'Keeffe is quite correct in stressing that in Frankfurt Tillich as a theologian was quite distinct from the *Institut*. But I do not think he is correct in de-emphasizing the influence of the members of the *Institut* on Tillich's thought.[39]

Economics was never of independent, isolated concern to Tillich. The discipline was of importance as related to humanistic needs, and the ethical and psychological implications of economics interested Tillich. Tillich stood in debt to both Marx and Freud and, like his friend Herbert Marcuse, these perspectives were synthesized into his own. An example of the tensions in thought produced by this synthesizing is available for examination in *The Protestant Era*.[40] On one page, he wrote:

> The economic sphere is the most important historical factor—not in all times, as some dogmatic Marxists assert—but certainly within bourgeois capitalism.[41]

However, on the very next page, his psychological interest became apparent:

> But more important than the immediate economic consequences of

---

[39] For a perspective critical of the work of John Stumme, Guy Hammond, and myself on the *Institut* influence on Tillich, see Terence O'Keeffe, "Tillich and the Frankfurt School," in *Theonomy and Autonomy*, ed. John J. Carey (Macon: Mercer University Press, 1984), 67-87.

[40] The references are to the original edition of *The Protestant Era* (Chicago: The University of Chicago Press, 1948). The later edition was abridged, and in the process, the last three chapters, the most limited to the immediate post-war scene and the most socialist, were eliminated.

[41] Tillich, *Protestant Era*, 239.

> the monopolistic stage of liberal economy are its psychological effects on the masses.[42]

The two claims for importance do not contradict each other, but they show the tension between a Marxist claim for the centrality of economics and a tendency to focus on the psychological state of the masses. He clamed the situation of the masses in the Western world created a revolutionary situation. This bearing of the tension between psychological and economic sources of political change is characteristic of Tillich and his friends associated with the critical theory of the Frankfurt School. It is not necessarily an anti-Marxist move in scholarship, since some today would regard it as a proper development of Marx's own insights. But such work, before the views of Fromm and Marcuse were widely known, was quite radical and controversial.

In response to Clark A. Kucheman's critical essay on Tillich's socialism from a capitalist perspective, Tillich again indicated the subordination of economics to humanist concerns in his thought.

> In the most extended description of my social-political ideas, the book *Die Sozialistische Entscheidung*, I have developed a many-sided image of a transformed society in which the economic element is definitively subordinated.[43]

His ideas about economics can only be grasped in his broadened humanistic perspective. In his view of a transformed order, which is basically socialist, some feudal and bourgeois elements remain.

Certain ideas about the economic order which were Marxist in inspiration were reduced in his writing and speaking after World War II. These ideas are present in the original edition of *The Protestant Era*, but absent or muted in the abridged edition. The social context in which he worked was different, and the "controlled

---

[42] Tillich, 240.

[43] Paul Tillich, "Rejoinder," *The Journal of Religion* 46 (January 1966), 190.

capitalism" of the United States, with its powerful trade unionist movement, was not the Berlin of the interwar period. The concept of the proletariat was obsolete in the United States. The problems of social injustice in the United States, primarily those of poverty and race, were problems of dehumanization which were not best addressed by the categories of early twentieth century German religious socialism. It seemed irrelevant to contend in the United States that (1) the masses were becoming more impoverished, or (2) that the increase of "unproductive capital in the banks"[44] drove the country into imperialism and war, or (3) that the rapidity of technological advance demanded by capitalism would necessarily mean increasing structural unemployment, or (4) that the proletariat were a revolutionary vanguard. However, the weakening of the persuasiveness of some of Marx's economic ideas did not allow his thought to be confined to the past. It had influenced modern thinking to the extent that an analysis of capitalist society, without reference to his thought, was unlikely to be productive. Tillich did not want to return to the illusions of harmony in the marketplace or justify contemporary democracies on the basis of an idealism of progress.[45]

Tillich knew the extent to which the workers of the Berlin suburbs were reduced in many aspects of their being to a mass level. The system of production, which included a standardization of work, a standardization of a low wage, a uniformity of housing opportunities, and a sameness of education to prepare them for industry determined their lives. He thought Marx was right in emphasizing that the system of material production was fundamental. However, he criticized Marxists who would simply deduce all aspects of culture from the system of production. To the extent that Marx rigidly deduced the superstructure from the substructure of production, Tillich was critical of his theory, also. For Tillich,

[44] Tillich, *Protestant Era*, 224.
[45] Tillich, 260.

> The economic sphere is itself a complex sphere, to which all other spheres essentially contribute, so that they cannot be derived from it, although they can never be separated from it.[46]

In economics, as elsewhere, his direct dependence on members of his discussion circle was acknowledged. Edward Heimann and Adolf Löwe, who had been members of his Kairos Circle in Berlin, for example, were the mentors of the economic theory in *The Socialist Decision*. The setting of economic reflections in the broad social context was a characteristic of the Frankfurt School.

THE FELLOWSHIP OF SOCIAL CHRISTIANS

The Niebuhr family had assisted in Tillich's transition from Frankfurt to New York. So his transition into the Niebuhr influenced Fellowship of Social Christians was one inevitable consequence of his move to New York City. When Tillich considered moving to Manchester, England, to join his colleague Adolf Löwe, Reinhold Niebuhr prevailed upon him to remain at Union so that they could found a school of theology there. They shared more in common in their social ethics than they did in their theology. They both were Christian realists, and until World War II, both were socialists.

Tillich joined the group which had functioned earlier under different names. The fellowship became better known when it began publishing *Radical Religion* in 1935.[47] The fellowship evolved, with Niebuhr's leadership remaining a constant as it changed its name to the Frontier Fellowship and then to Christian Action in September 1951. The Christian Action form of the society had "850 members in 42 states and 9 countries" in 1954.48 Its projects included support for the Southern Tenant Farmers Union and the founding, funding,

[46] Tillich, 258.

[47] John C. Bennett, "Tillich and the Fellowship of Socialist Christians," *North American Paul Tillich Society Newsletter* 16 (October 1980), 3.

[48] Reinhold Niebuhr, "The Significance of the Growth of Christian Action," *Christianity and Crisis* 14, no. 4 (March 22, 1954), 30

and support of the interracial Delta Cooperative Farm in Mississippi before the civil rights movement of the 1950s.

The central supporters of the Fellowship of Social Christians and *Radical Religion* in its earliest days were Reinhold Niebuhr, Winnifred Wygal, Eduard Heimann, Joseph F. Fletcher, Sherwood Eddy, Paul Tillich, John C. Bennett, Harry Bone, and Rose Terlin. The work of the fellowship was that of social theology, and its political and economic commitments were in terms of socialism. The group was non-communist but understood itself to be in debt to Karl Marx in terms of social philosophy, if not in metaphysics. The editor's philosophy included, in 1943, a program of socialization of major centers of property.

> It is quite obvious that these forms of "private" property which represent primarily social power, and the most potent social power of our day at that, cannot remain in private hands. The socialization of such property is a *sine qua non* of social justice.[49]

The earliest form of the society regarded Christian ethics as being in direct conflict with the ethos of capitalist individualism and its structures. The groups recognized the class struggle and called for "the aggressive assertion of the rights of the exploited and the disinherited." They hoped that class warfare could be avoided by all classes coming to recognize the need for radical social change. This position recognized the "covert and overt violence inherent in the present order."[50]

The declaration of objectives called for the application of Christian ethics to individual lives, to unite radical groups within the churches to strengthen their socialist influence, to encourage revolutionary social change, and to help the radical social movement to be more infused with "the religious spirit."

---

[49] A.T. Mollegen, "The Common Convictions of the Fellowship of Socialist Christians," *Christianity and Society* (Spring 1943), 28.

[50] Mollegen, "The Fellowship of Socialist Christians," reprinted in *Radical Religion* (Winter 1973), 7.

Members were obligated to take on Christian socialist discipline for social action and witness, including joining labor unions, organizing within their churches, joining in public social conflicts nonviolently, supporting socialist political parties, and paying on a "graded tax schedule" for causes that supported the aims of the "cooperative commonwealth" and the Society. The "graded tax schedule" was highly progressive and required as contribution all the net taxable income of a family beyond $8,000. These taxes were eventually dropped as being overly legalistic.

Much of the work of the society retreats and publications was theological. Both Tillich and Niebuhr were writing their major theological works during the time of the society's life.[51] John Bennett listed five areas that he remembered as the major emphases of political-economic discussion in the society: (1) The continued evaluation of Soviet communism through the late 1930s, (2) response to the rise of fascism (both Tillich and Heimann were refugees from Nazism), (3) response to World War II, (4) the movement away from the Socialist Party to the New Deal with Niebuhr himself campaigning for Franklin D. Roosevelt in the closing days of the 1936 campaign,[52] and (5) evolution in the thought about socialism. A.T. Mollegen's summary of 1943 had described the society as supporting autonomous public agencies like TVA, cooperatives, socialization of centers of economic power, and organized labor.[53]

In the closing years of the fellowship, as it merged into Christian Action, the membership grew to 1,200 and there were about a dozen local chapters. Much of the new organization's energy was put into combating the McCarthy movement and spirit in the early

---

[51] Bennett, "Tillich and the Fellowship," 3.

[52] Conversation with Charles Brown (June 2, 1991), who presented evidence from Richard Fox, *Reinhold Niebuhr* (New York: Pantheon Books, 1985), 177-78 and independent confirmations of those who heard him speak.

[53] The five points are summarized in Bennett, "Tillich and the Fellowship," 3-5.

1950s. Effort was also made to distinguish Christian social action from Marxism. Other foes that received critiques were the various movements trying to synthesize capitalist individualism and Christianity. The group also encouraged a positive relationship between Christian faith and democratic political participation, and they seemed to prevail in clarifying that issue[54] until the rise of the religious right.

Though Tillich was closer personally to Wilhelm Pauck, in matters political he allied with his colleagues John Bennett and Reinhold Niebuhr. On one occasion he dropped a note to John Bennett requesting his political advice, writing, "What shall I do? You are my father confessor in politics and religion!"[55] Tillich did not shift as far away from religious socialism as Niebuhr. In 1955 he left the group as he moved to Harvard. He summarized the group's evolution noting that Niebuhr had changed the most, with Eduard Heimann, his old friend from Berlin, close behind. Tillich thought he had changed less and John Bennett even less so. He indicated the need to join psychological insights to sociological ones to understand and resist the pressures of mass society. He noted that the group as a whole no longer trusted the socialist analysis while it still struggled politically for fragmentary realizations of the Kingdom. He celebrated the fellowship and closed by exhorting the group to continue the prophetic spirit, but to "Do it better!"[56]

The leaders of Christian Action were involved in many other similar causes, in their denominations and in the ecumenical movement. Niebuhr was unable to give it as much energy after his 1952

---

[54] Robert T. Handy, "Christian Action in Perspective," *Christianity and Society* 21 (Summer 1956), 10-14.

[55] Letter from Tillich to Bennett, August 18, 1959. Copy in author's collection.

[56] Paul Tillich, "Past and Present Reflections on Christianity and Society," May 1955, 4, unpublished typescript, Paul Tillich Papers, Andover-Harvard Theological Library, Cambridge.

stroke. The burden of financing a national office detracted from the work. Denominations were evolving their own social action programs, and the National Council of Churches was promising a vital program in social analysis and action. All these factors combined with a conviction that fresh analysis of the political economy was needed rather than the continued application of a fading Christian socialist consensus. *Christianity and Society* was discontinued in the summer of 1956, after the national office of Christian Action was closed in February. For about twenty years these ventures of publication, fellowship, study, and support of social action had received Niebuhr's support. They also had drawn the Union Theological students into expressions of social thought and action and become part of their education. During Niebuhr's lifetime, the intellectual legacy was continued by *Christianity and Crisis* while the political work was directed into Americans for Democratic Action and the Liberal Party. The mainline church expanding social action and education programs and staffs also continued much of the work of the fellowship. Tillich's organizational work faded as he left Union and pushed to complete his *Systematic Theology*.

Chapter 3

TILLICH AND NIEBUHR ON THE JEWISH QUESTION[1]

Paul Tillich recorded in his *Travel Diary: 1936* his warm associations with Niebuhr in Geneva. They breakfasted together, lunched together by the lake, and worked on lectures together. Tillich translated Niebuhr's lecture, and they reflected together on European politics at that fateful hour. Tillich remembered asking Niebuhr about academic positions at Ann Arbor and Manchester, England. He recorded that Niebuhr advised him to stay at Union Theological Seminary and "We will found a school of theology there." He noted in his reflection for July 30: "I have a feeling of warmth with him such as I had never experienced before."[2]

They were at their closest intellectually when they were working on questions of religion and society. Tillich's faithful realism and

---

[1] This chapter was published originally in the *North American Paul Tillich Society Newsletter* 20, no. 2 (April 1994): 2-8.

[63] Paul Tillich, *My Travel Diary: 1936* (New York: Harper & Row Publishers, 1970), 145.

Niebuhr's Christian realism bound them together to support religious socialism during the 1930s. Niebuhr's movement away from socialism in the 1940s led Tillich and Niebuhr to diverge politically. But the impossibility of Tillich carrying religious socialism forward in the Eisenhower years meant their divergences were not widely known. For years they shared The Fellowship of Socialist Christians.[3] They also shared teaching responsibilities in "Philosophy of Religion" at Union Theological Seminary, while Niebuhr also taught "Christian Ethics" and Tillich, "Systematic Theology." Tillich wrote appreciatively of Ursula Niebuhr's welcoming them to Union Theological Seminary the day they arrived in New York as well as his debt to Reinhold for conveying the offer to come to Union after he was dismissed in Frankfurt. But despite friendships and three decades of shared scholarly and political causes, no one at Union could have regarded them as sharing a school of theology. On the other hand, by their greatness they did contribute to strengthening Union and increasing its importance, so they did strengthen a school.

The differences between them became clearer with the publication of *The Systematic Theology* in 1951. The end of religious socialist commitments occurred roughly at the same time as the differences between them as representatives of biblically based pragmatism and ontologically developed existentialism became clearer.

Roger Shinn, as a student of both Paulus and Reinie, has put this divergence as clearly as anyone:

> When Tillich arrived in this country, knowing no English, Reinie was one person with whom he could converse. As late as my time, I heard them occasionally exchange comments, in German, as they passed each other in the halls. Each had a genuine admiration for the other. See Gilkey's angry review of Fox for an example of Tillich's admiration for Reinie. Many people glibly associated the two as "neo-orthodox," a bad categorization for both. I think I once

---

[64] See Bennett, "Tillich and the Fellowship," 4, 3.

> wrote in *C&C*, back in the days when I was one of their regulars that I long puzzled over this categorization of Tillich until the reason dawned on me: he spoke with a German accent. There's one other possible reason: As Niebuhr once said in a friendly, jovial way, "Whatever heresies Paul Tillich goes wandering among, he always comes home to 'justification by faith."

But to back up, the two became strongly associated in the public mind. A second reason is that each of them defended the other against critics of the prevailing liberal-rational type. So the critics of both tended to merge them. The phrase, "Niebuhr-and-Tillich," became almost one word in some circles, even sometimes at Union. But it was foolish.

There was one more reason for the popular association. When Tillich arrived in this country, Niebuhr immediately welcomed him and many of his friends (including Eduard Heimann and others from the New School) into the Fellowship of Socialist Christians, and they there found something of an American base. Actually, as Tillich's book on religious socialism shows, there was a considerable difference between the continental group and Niebuhr's American group. But they shared many criticisms of the dominant American culture, and from the mainstream of American politics they looked alike.

> One night (somewhere in my 1945-49 period at Union) I found myself helping Reinie and Ursula clean up their kitchen after a party. We combined intellectual conversation with dishwashing in a very Niebuhrian way. Something led Reinie to comment, "You know, I've just begun to realize how really different Paul and I are." I replied brashly—it was easy to be brash around Reinie—"Your students have known it for a long time." He laughed in his friendly way. We students knew it because we were getting Tillich's "system" in his lectures; Niebuhr, reading Tillich's early publications and entering conversation with him, was slower in getting the

impact of "the system."[4]

Tillich's work had been called to Reinhold's attention by his brother. Tillich would, at a later date, credit H. Richard Niebuhr for saving his life by translating *The Religious Situation* and thereby winning an invitation for him to come to the US. Reinhold's reviews in 1932[5] and 1936[6] of Tillich's earliest translations into English were full of praise, as was his 1937[7] essay "The Contribution of Paul Tillich." These early pieces did not prefigure the later arguments; the last and major essay from the 1930s only raised a question about the need for more attention to the historical Jesus. He celebrated Paulus; after all he had sponsored his immigration.

> For he is not only one of the most brilliant theologians in the Western world, but one whose thought is strikingly relevant to every major problem of culture and civilization. His terms may be abstract, but his thought is not. It deals in terms of rigorous realism with the very stuff of life.[8]

Tillich's review of Niebuhr's *Nature and Destiny of Man* returned the compliments and raised questions primarily about historical judgments and some of Niebuhr's comparisons. He called it a masterpiece of theology and applauded its chapters on sin.

Niebuhr's critique of Tillich in the Charles Kegley and Robert Bretall essay collection moved their discussion into the deeper areas

---

[4] Roger Shinn, letter responding to Ronald Stone's Questionnaire (November 1990). The letter is in author's possession.

[5] Reinhold Niebuhr, "Review of *The Religious Situation*," *The World Tomorrow* 15, no. 23 (December 21, 1932), 596.

[6] Reinhold Niebuhr, "Review of *Interpretation of History*," *Radical Religion* 2 (Winter 1936): 41-42.

[7] Reinhold Niebuhr, "The Contribution of Paul Tillich," *Religion in Life* 6, no. 4 (Autumn 1937): 574-81.

[8] Niebuhr, "Contribution," 581.

of disagreement.[9] Until the end, Niebuhr remained suspicious of Tillich's ontology. He wanted to preserve poetic-dramatic language concerning the human condition and he feared Tillich's language reduced both human responsibility and the difference between their positions. Niebuhr would concede an implicit ontology in interpretations of Biblical insight and in the Bible itself, but he wanted to keep the ontology implicit. Tillich wanted to make it explicit, and Niebuhr called such explication speculation. Tillich was certainly correct in asking for more careful definitions. Niebuhr feared too much precision over systematized faith reduced mystery which was important to his sense of the Christian faith. More than that, he feared that Tillich's understanding of estrangement made human sin more subject to fate and less to responsibility than he believed the human situation warranted. Niebuhr's critique of Tillich was at its strongest in this pre-stroke essay. His later responses in a 1956 review of *Biblical Religion and the Search for Ultimate Reality*,[10] that was in part a response to Niebuhr's "Biblical Thought and Ontological Speculation,"[11] was weaker, as was his response to Tillich's criticism in Charles Kegley and Robert Bretall's Niebuhr volume.[12] Tillich kept up the attack in the Harold Landon volume, *Reinhold Niebuhr:*

---

[9] Reinhold Niebuhr, "Biblical Thought and Ontological Speculation in Tillich's Theology," in *The Theology of Paul Tillich*, eds. Charles W. Kegley and Robert W. Bretall (New York: Macmillan, 1952), 216-27.

[10] Reinhold Niebuhr, "Review of *Biblical Religion and the Search for Ultimate* Reality," *Union Seminary Quarterly Review* 11, no. 2 (January 1956): 59-60.

[11] Niebuhr, "Biblical Thought and Ontological Speculation," 216-27.

[12] Reinhold Niebuhr, "Reply to Interpretation and Criticism, By Reinhold Niebuhr," in *Reinhold Niebuhr: His Religious, Social, and Political Thought*, eds. Charles W. Kegley and Robert W. Bretall (New York: Macmillan, 1961): 429-51.

A Prophetic Voice in Our Time.[13] While confessing his indebtedness to Niebuhr and his appreciation for their life long conversation, he criticized him relentlessly for not turning to ontology. He criticized him first for taking philosophic opinions out of context and out of time and finding them to be in error in comparison to Biblical views. He tried to suggest that Niebuhr was accepting of *universal estrangement* as descriptive of the human condition. He urged Niebuhr to use ontology in thinking about freedom and destiny, pride, and self. In Niebuhr's response he merely suggested he preferred not to use Plotinus' concepts and that he now preferred to use the symbols descriptively rather than ontologically.[14] At that point in the argument, Tillich had certainly won. But the resultant discussion by their common friends and colleagues denied Tillich the victory. John Hutchison, Wilhelm Pauck, and Richard Kroner all defended Niebuhr's right to use his terms without needing to use Tillich's ontology. My own reading of the debate is that Tillich was correct to push Niebuhr for more careful definition of his terms and very mistaken in thinking this meant he should use Tillich's terms. In these exchanges they both were careful to say how they appreciated the realism of the other's position.

They kept most of their disagreements private, though an exchange about the religious meaning of Picasso's *Guernica* broke into the open.[15] In correspondence, Niebuhr would recognize Tillich as

---

[13] Paul Tillich, "Sin and Grace in the Theology of Reinhold Niebuhr," in *Reinhold Niebuhr: A Prophetic Voice in Our Time*, ed. Harold Landon (Greenwich: Seabury Press, 1962): 27-41.

[14] Reinhold Niebuhr, "The Response of Reinhold Niebuhr," in *Reinhold Niebuhr: A Prophetic Voice in Our Time*, ed. Harold Landon (Greenwich: Seabury Press, 1962), 120.

[15] Reinhold Niebuhr, "Editorial Notes," *Christianity and Crisis* 16, no. 1 (February 6, 1956): 2-3; Paul Tillich, "To the Editor," *Christianity and Crisis* 16, no. 3 (March 5, 1956): 24.

the greater theologian,[16] and Tillich, in The Fellowship of Socialist Christians would recognize Niebuhr as the genius in political thought.[17]

The most famous difference between them, of course, was the anecdotal gap between them on the appreciation of nature. Tillich referred to it as Niebuhr accusing him of being a German romanticist as he appreciated a tree in Riverside Park. Other students' versions have Niebuhr referring to him as a damned nature mystic or of Tillich quoting Niebuhr's rumored description of him as such when Niebuhr asked him why he stopped either in front of a tree in Riverside Park or the flowers in the Union quadrangle. In dialogue with Zen Buddhists, Tillich described himself as a nature mystic.

CHRISTIAN ZIONISM

The meaning of the term Zionism varied according to the positions of those claiming to be Zionists. The meaning of the term Christian also has different meanings. The use of Christian as an adjective modifying Zionism seems peculiar as Zionism is a Jewish movement. Here in reference to Reinhold Niebuhr and Paul Tillich it means that they come to support the establishment of a "Jewish state" in Israel as Christian theologians. As a Jew can be a Zionist without migrating to Israel or a Christian may be a Christian-Marxist without subscribing to the metaphysics of Karl Marx, so it is possible for a Christian to be a Zionist in the sense of supporting Jewish migration to Israel and the consolidation of the Jewish people into a state. Following contemporary usage, Zionism implies more than the "national homeland" of the Balfour declaration, and it is not reconcilable with the "unitary, non-sectarian state" of E1 Fatah.

---

[16] Letter of Reinhold Niebuhr to Will Scarlett, 5 November 1968, Washington papers of Reinhold Niebuhr, Library of Congress.

[17] Langdon Gilkey, "A Critical Review Article" (unpublished manuscript, August 1987), 24. The draft is in author's possession.

> *Zionism* may be summarily defined as the Jewish nationalist movement whose endeavors to solve the "Jewish problem" led to the establishment of the "Jewish state" of Israel.[18]

It is not self-evident that American theologians would be Christians in support of Zionism. None of the major church positions could really be regarded as Zionist, though they accept Israel. The tendency of the Christian archaeological community which has worked in Jordan, the American missionary interests, liberation theologians, and official church boards to be pro-Palestinian and slightly hostile to Israel policy is, I think, generally recognized.

FRIENDSHIPS WITH AND RESPECT FOR JEWS

Niebuhr and Tillich found themselves forming close friendships with Jews who were allied in struggling for social justice. Both of them had grown up in parsonages of German parentage, Niebuhr in Missouri and Illinois and Tillich in Eastern Germany and Berlin. Tillich remembered that though anti-Semitism had been discussed in his home, it had been rejected by his parents. Neither, as youth, of course, was free from the anti-Judaism sentiments which their church contexts encouraged. As an adult, Tillich remarked that as a young boy, particularly during Holy Week, he found the anti-Judaism teaching of the church impressed upon him. Reinhold Niebuhr recorded how as a young boy he observed the stereotyping of Jewish businessmen in his Midwestern town. The generous, courteous Jewish merchant was thought of by the gentiles as atypical; the prosperous, rather pushy Jewish capitalist was regarded as typical. As a young boy who knew few Jews, he had no basis for ignoring or judging such stereotyping.

Their friendships with Jews that are documented are post-World War I. In his last book Niebuhr documented the importance

[18] Ben Halpern, "Zionism," in *International Encyclopedia of the Social Sciences*, eds. David L. Sills and Robert K. Merton (New York: The Macmillan Co., 1968), 593.

of his friendship in Detroit with Fred Butzel. Niebuhr liked to quote his mentor, the Episcopalian Bishop Charles Williams, a follower of the social gospel who said, "In the weightier matters of social justice there are only two Christians in Detroit, and they are both Jews."[19] Niebuhr reflected on the sources of the social-righteousness he perceived among Jews. He thought that perhaps it should be attributed to the prophetic tradition. He noted that many of the most religious Jews attributed it to the *Torah*. Butzel, however, who had served with Niebuhr on the Mayor's Race Committee, attributed the passion for social righteousness to their minority status which resulted in suspicion of the establishment and compassion for other minorities. Niebuhr never resolved the issue in his own mind but noted that Butzel's genius was responsible for the beginning of "my long love affair with the Jewish people."[20] His respect for the Jews had led him in an early article to contrast their concern for social justice with the relative impotence of German-Americans in supporting any progressive causes. The superiority of Jewish social sensitivity to most Protestant social consciousness was to remain a theme throughout Niebuhr's teaching and writing. The urban pastoral of Detroit was essential to developing Niebuhr's own social realism, and part of that mixture was his debt to Jewish friends.

Tillich was in Berlin during the 1918 revolution. He spoke at radical political rallies, attempted to move the church to revolutionize its own traditions, and lectured on social problems at the University of Berlin. Soon he found himself evolving as a leader of a small discussion group of intellectuals for religious socialism. The group which became known as the Kairos Circle, after Tillich's use of the concept, included Jews, notably Eduard Heimann and Adolf Löwe. They taught the young Christian theologian economics and implanted their influence in his social philosophy. They were to

---

[19] Reinhold Niebuhr, *Man's Nature and His Communities* (New York: Charles Scribner's Sons, 1965), 18.

[20] Niebuhr, 19.

continue his close friends throughout his life, sharing his exile, his wine, and helping to shape his mind. The context of his friendships with Jews is different than Niebuhr's but also similar in pressing social conflicts, alliances with Jewish leaders, and resulting friendships.

Tillich, as Dean of the philosophy faculty, was at the center of the struggle for the University of Frankfurt. When storm troopers attacked Jewish students, he took them to his office for protection and medical aid. He demanded in print the expulsion of students who joined the storm troopers. He was attacked in the *Frankfurter Zeitung*, and passages from his *The Socialist Decision* were quoted to prove him an enemy of the new order. He was suspended from his post on April 13, 1933; further consultations with the ministry of education, at which Tillich pushed questions concerning governmental attitudes toward Jews and modern culture, proved that Tillich's academic career in Germany was over.

Meanwhile, Reinhold Niebuhr had been visiting Germany. He had gotten in an argument with the pastor of his German relatives over the pastor's anti-Semitism and created tension at the family reunion. Niebuhr telephoned Tillich of the offer for him to come to Union Theological Seminary as a visiting faculty member. Eventually, after a near arrest by the Gestapo, Tillich came to New York.

These Jewish friends of Niebuhr and Tillich were not necessarily Zionists, but the friendships laid the ground for a deep emphatic reaction to the Holocaust and the founding of Israel. Before Herbert Marcuse moved to California, he was often present at Tillich's apartment as were other Jewish friends from the Berlin and Frankfurt days. In later years Abraham Heschel and Reinhold Niebuhr formed a close friendship which had a mutual influence on each other's thought. Gradually, traffic between Jewish Theological Seminary and Union Theological Seminary across Broadway increased as mutual trust and respect between their institutions deepened. I know from my own experience how differently I have viewed Judaism and the need to save Soviet Jewry after forming friendships with Jews on an Americans for Democratic Action tour of the Soviet Union. Friendships, particularly friendships formed in the context of the struggle for social justice, may be the most important aspect of Jewish-Christian dialogue.

SOCIAL ETHICS

The developed political philosophies of Niebuhr and Tillich were both socialist and democratic. They remained socialist inspired even after the socialist option was destroyed in Germany and proved politically barren in the United States. Israel, when it emerged, gave every promise of being the most socialist and the most democratic state in the Middle East. This affinity between their goals and the announced goals of the new state made their support natural.

Both political philosophies recognized politics as the struggle for power. Neither was blinded by illusions that states simply pursued a moral cause. They were open to the ambiguity of politics in the Middle East and neither had to reject Israel on moralistic grounds just as they had not rejected the British mandate on moralistic grounds. Niebuhr spoke of pure justice as always being compromised by the pursuit of interests, and a rough justice as being the harmonization of competing interests. For Tillich, justice was the state of affairs that would allow the relative power of different centers to flourish without crushing each other. Both Christian moralists also recognized that most borders were created in conflict and so they were not subject to the sort of Christian or liberal moralism which proclaims that no borders established through war are to be recognized, as Security Council Resolution 242 (1967) implies. Their values of democratic procedures, respect for civil rights, need for social planning, and realism combined to make them potential supporters of Israel.

Another strain of these political thinkers reinforced the above values to incline them to respect Jewish developments in the land of Israel. Both thinkers relied heavily on the Hebrew prophets in their preaching and teaching. More fundamental, however, was the use of prophetic religion to describe their social theology. They intended that history be taken seriously but not absolutely. They pleaded for active political involvement of a progressive sort that eschewed all fanaticisms and determinisms. Their sympathies for some of Marx's social thought rested on their detection of genuinely prophetic elements within his own social thought. Their respect for the Hebrew prophets was so great that the term prophet is perhaps the best single tribute to Reinhold Niebuhr. He read the contingent in terms of the eternal and fought and pled for justice. The socialist journal that Niebuhr founded, *Radical Religion*, understood itself to be representing the prophetic spirit under the conditions of the twentieth century. Doom was pronounced on the tottering house of capitalism, and justice was demanded in the name of God. Like another prophet before him, Niebuhr was perhaps surprised when Nineveh repented and was spared. He changed with the times, however, and with the old capitalism dying under the pragmatic adjustments of the New Deal, he became a defender of the mixed economy or social-welfare capitalism. He remained on the left in encouraging the powers of the state to be used for the disadvantaged.

TILLICH'S SOCIALISM

The explicit connections between prophetic religion and social criticism are perhaps best seen in Tillich's major work on social theory, *The Socialist Decision* (1933). This volume was written in 1932 to fight the threat of National Socialism. It was banned in 1933 soon after Hitler assumed power. Though it circulated in the underground, most of the printed volumes of it were destroyed when American bombers destroyed the warehouse in which they were stored. *The Socialist Decision* is a work of speculative, critical, political philosophy directed against Nazism. In the work he proposes a reformulation of socialism so that it can more effectively combat Nazism.

For Tillich there are basically two types of political philosophy. They are either grounded in myths of origin or in the prophetic criticism of myths of origin. Political romanticisms (read conservatism and Nazism) are attempts to define political existence as sacred because of its origins in soil, blood, or race. Western capitalism, on the other hand, is an expression of the attacks on the myths of origin. Western capitalism, riding the waves of the enlightenment and bourgeois revolt, broke the social order of feudalism grounded in myths of origin. It was not, however, able to establish harmony. Its rational, controlling mentality could destroy but not replace the sense of order and purpose of the social order of feudalism. Political romanticism attacked capitalism in the name of the powers of origin: blood, soil, and group. Socialism attacked capitalism from within and shared some of the weaknesses it sought to overcome. If socialism as rational social planning were to prevail, it had to reform itself and take on some of the strengths of conservatism and political romanticism. The chaos of contemporary Germany required new answers which conservatism could not give, and political romanticism was only a destructive movement with no lasting power to govern. Socialism, like capitalism, inherited the motif of prophetic criticism which could surrender to neither social-resignation nor utopia, but it needed to unite its social planning with symbols of expectation to change society. To achieve this, socialism had to affirm its religious dimensions and to demonstrate that it had a place for appreciation of the national homeland as well as internationalism, the family as well as society, traditional organizations as well as rational planning.

Tillich criticized Nazism's pretensions to be scientific. While admitting its philosophy was powerful poetry tending toward ecstatic and revolutionary apocalyptic, he dismissed it as a serious school of thought. It was a demonic movement in its attempt to make sacred leader, race, party, and space. The only integrity for the church was to oppose Nazism. Nazism was understood as an alternative religious attempt to create a system of meaning and solution by a leap back to myths of origin without critical inquiry.

The spirit of Nazism was essentially opposed to the spirit of Judaism. The spirit of Judaism was located in the worship of the God who transcended blood, soil, and communal loyalties and demanded justice. The pagan myths of origin were broken in the Hebrew Bible, and so the Old Testament was opposed by Nazism. The spirit of Judaism was eternally an adversary to the spirit of political romanticism. Myths of origin could still be found in biblical Jewish faith but only in a criticized mode. Christianity and especially the churches of the reformation had to join with Judaism in the affirmation of the prophetic critique of romanticism. The political romanticism of Nazism was a counter-movement against the prophetic in religion and humanism in culture. In Judaism these primitive notions of blood and race found a sharp intellectual critique.

Tillich's critique included socialism which neglected its prophetic heritage and so lacked the power of expectation. A rediscovery of eschatology would, he thought, show socialism how it could reform its ideology. There were imminent possibilities within the proletariat which had to be emphasized in a call for the transformation of the human situation. In fact, for Tillich the essence of the socialist principle is the principle of expectation or political eschatology. The essential point for the argument is that Tillich found in the Hebrew prophets a political eschatology which was necessary for the reform of socialism and to save Germany and the world from the barbarism of the Nazi movement. However, 1933 was too late; socialism was exhausted, capitalism was disgraced and fragmented, conservatism was irrelevant, and chaos and war resulted.

In New York, Tillich and Niebuhr joined with Jewish friends in organizing relief programs for exiles from Germany and joined in criticizing anti-Semitism. After becoming an American citizen, Tillich spoke publicly at political rallies as Niebuhr was doing consistently. His first public speech against the regime in Germany at

Madison Square Garden attacked its anti-Semitism. When Tillich began a series of propaganda broadcasts for the Voice of America, his first one, on March 31, 1942, was addressed to *Meine deutschen Freunde* on "The Jewish Question." He addressed himself primarily to German-Protestant church people. He pointed out that the religion of Protestant Christians is of Jewish origin. The Old Testament is part of the Christian Bible and the reformation was founded in the name and spirit of the Jewish Paul. An attack on Judaism was a surrender of Christianity, and all Christians, he argued, were obligated to defend Jewish people resolutely. The persecution of the Jews was blasphemy and opposition to God. So, throughout his wartime broadcasting dealing with a variety of political and philosophical issues he returned to attack anti-Semitism.

Niebuhr's arguments for a Jewish homeland appeared in *The Nation* in 1942.[21] Recognizing Judaism as a nationality as well as a cultural and religious group, he argued for a homeland after the holocaust. He regarded it as a solution to be contained within British imperial policy and American foreign policy as part of the post-war settlement. Arguments for Jewish rights were set in the context of the need for settlement of Arab claims. He criticized Zionist claims that there would be no "injustices" to Arabs, but he hoped for an overall settlement which would compensate for losses. These articles and articles by others in his *Christianity and Crisis* set him against the anti-Zionist policies of *The Christian Century* and the immediate past and then presidents of Union Theological Seminary.

The increase in their Zionist militancy was reflected in the formation of the Christian Council on Palestine in mid-1942. Paul Tillich and Reinhold Niebuhr were joined by three others as the executive committee. Between 1942 and 1946, when it merged into the American Christian Palestine Committee, it recruited three

[21] Reinhold Niebuhr, "Jews after the War," *The Nation* (February 21, 1942): 214-6, 253-5.

thousand American clergymen to subscribe to its pro-Zionist principles. In the preface to Waldo Frank's book, *The Jew in Our Day*, Niebuhr argued for political security for the Jews in Palestine "without reference to the final religious problem."[22] Fishman has detailed the political intrigues of these Christian Zionists during the war.[23] Carl Voss, the secretary of the Council, was in the process of writing a book on this story when he died.

When the Anglo-American Committee of Inquiry held hearings in Washington, D.C., Niebuhr testified for the Christian Council in Palestine on January 14, 1946. He argued for a Jewish state and more openness to Jewish immigration in Palestine. The final report of the Committee essentially agreed as did President Truman, but the British government referred the issue to the United Nations in 1947.

The similarities in the writing of Tillich and Niebuhr on Judaism are striking. They rejected aggressive mission to convert Jews to Christianity. They continued the dialogue with Jewish friends, and they expressed a willingness to help Jews who were alienated from Judaism to find meaning in Christianity. They affirmed the need of preserving Judaism against tendencies in Christianity to relapse into paganism.

During the war they both called for the defeat of Germany and urged Western nations to secure the safety of the Jews. They urged distinctions between the guilt of the regime and the guilt of the German people. Both sought to encourage forces in Germany which could act against Hitler and urged restraint in the practice of war and for policies which would encourage resistance to mount within Germany. They recognized the need for a homeland for the Jewish people, but they were not absolutist about the need for it to be in Israel. As with other Zionists, they debated other options. The

---

[22] Hertzel Fishman, *American Protestantism and a Jewish State* (Detroit: Wayne State University Press, 1973), 75.

[23] Fishman, 75.

establishment of Israel in 1948 they accepted as fact. Israel was the response to the Holocaust. For them the two are historically tied together. Niebuhr would comment on each of Israel's wars revealing both his love for Israel and his stance against Arab politics. With the aid of secular and religious Jews he founded Americans for Democratic Action which continued political support for Israel among American liberals.

ANTI-SEMITISM AND ZIONISM

Tillich analyzed German guilt for World War II activities against the Jews in 1953 in Berlin. Though he knew Germans did not want to think about their guilt, he regarded it as of the first importance for Germans to come to grip with guilt. The primary guilt lay upon those directly responsible for the atrocities and, of course, only some Germans were so responsible. A secondary type of guilt derived from failure to act responsibly, and he affirmed that he was guilty of not acting more boldly as the German political situation deteriorated in 1932-33. Most Germans he thought participated in some of the other three types of guilt: the guilt of suppressing knowledge, the guilt of forgetting of one's responsibility for the past, and the guilt of regarding the past as over with no consequences for the present. He regarded the guilt that was troubling Germany as operating at psychological depths in much of the population. He urged the recognition of the guilt and that positive steps be taken to deal with it.

In dealing with Christian anti-Semitism he also used his analysis of five types of guilt. In regard to the question of the guilt of Jews for the death of Jesus, he found none of the types of guilt applicable. The accusation that Jews were guilty for the death of Jesus was absurd. His program to free the churches from anti-Semitism involved the following: the review of church publications to purge them of dangerous stereotypes; the emphasis on the Old Testament in the church; the abandonment of the active missionary movement to Jews; the sharing of worship services; the alliance for the struggle for social justice; theological dialogue; and the acceptance of the continuity and authenticity of Jewish faith. The primary witness of the power of Christ to Judaism would be in the demonstration of the quality of life in Christianity which would eradicate the demon of anti-Semitism in the life of the church.

Tillich had known Judaism as the faith of a dispersed people without a land for most of his life. His acceptance of a pro-Zionist position was after the fact of the establishment of Israel. He joined the American Christian Palestine Committee which promoted sympathy for Israel in the US. In explaining his pro-Zionist position he reported how his own position had changed. His earlier teaching that Israel was a people of time without attachment to space was mistaken, he said. Europe was not a secure haven for the Jews; they had to have their own place where they could protect themselves. Assimilation of the Jews in European culture had been a disaster; they had to find their own way. The average Jew was not a prophetic figure who should suffer in dispersion for the world; she was just a person who needed protection.

He accepted Israel as a state, not as fulfillment of a Biblical promise. The state of Israel had to be judged as other nations were judged. Israel was a necessary refuge for the survivors of the Holocaust and other expressions of anti-Judaism. His recommendations and hopes for Israel were parallel to his advice to Germans: accept finite borders and develop a sense of national-vocational consciousness within these borders. There is no absolute security; all borders will have some insecurity. Security rests in accepted borders and international understanding across the borders. Solutions will be found through negotiation and compromise that recognize the rights and power of all parties to the dispute.

For Niebuhr, Israel was primarily a refuge for the victims of the Holocaust. He regarded it as a responsibility of the United States to protect Israel for reasons of moral responsibility and for reasons of national interest. He wrote before the Israel-Egypt 1956 War:

> Our nation has a special interest in the preservation of the state of Israel. That interest is not only dictated by national interest in a state devoted to Western democracy and surrounded by Islamic nations in various stages of feudal decay, but is also dictated by humane considerations. For the state of Israel is, whatever its limitations, a heartening adventure in nationhood. It has gathered the Jews of all nations, the remnants of the victims of Hitlerism and other forms of nationalistic persecution, and given them a home of their own. Whatever our political or religious positions may be, it is not possible to withhold admiration, sympathy and respect for such an achievement.[24]

In writing on the strange mixture of secular and religious forces in the modern world he regarded the emergence of Israel "as a kind of penance of the world for the awful atrocities committed against the Jews."[25] Furthermore, he noted that injury was done to the Arabs, but still he wrote, "Many Christians are pro-Zionist in the sense that they believe a homeless people require a homeland."[26] Justice still required further work on the rights of the Palestinians.

Niebuhr's writing on Judaism in 1958 in *Pious and Secular America* and his last essay, "Mission and Opportunity: Religion in 'Pluralistic Culture'," in Louis Finkelstein's volume *Social Responsibility in an Age of Revolution* (1971), are among the most profound

[24] Reinhold Niebuhr, "New Hopes for Peace in the Middle East," *Christianity and Crisis* 16, no. 9 (May 28, 1956), 65.

[25] Reinhold Niebuhr, *Pious and Secular America* (New York: Charles Scribner's Sons, 1958), 109.

[26] Niebuhr, 109.

contributions to Christian-Jewish understanding.[27] In the context of the two religious contributions to ethics in the Western world, he recognizes that certain issues between the faiths are non-negotiable and he suggests ways in which both faiths can correct their traditions to promote understanding without proselytizing.

Tillich's death in 1965 and Niebuhr's in 1971 prevent us from knowing how their thought would have evolved vis-a-vis contemporary Israel. A few points are clear, however. Their Zionism did not mean that all Jews should live in Zion. Israel was of the diaspora as well as Eretz Israel. The creation of Israel was the recreation of a historical nation which was to be evaluated as other nations are evaluated. Israel has a religious history, and while it is relevant to the present state of Israel, it is not determinative. For Tillich and Niebuhr, history is radically free, and God judges all nations for their unrighteousness. To want to defend the Jewish choice to return to Israel after the Holocaust does not imply either Biblical or secular absolutism. It can be done on the basis that Jews were neither welcome nor secure elsewhere and that the international community of nations recognized the right of Israel to exist.

The genius of Israel does not depend upon the land but on its relationship to a transcendent God who always requires justice. In neither Tillich nor Niebuhr's thought can borders be regarded as sacrosanct. Borders get changed. They both recognized that our concern for security produces arrogance and blindness, but both recognized the need for security. Defense budgets can tyrannize a people, but people who will not provide for defense in a warring world would bear illusions that Jews cannot afford.

Neither theologian dealt adequately with the plight of Palestinians living within Israel, nor did either address themselves at length to the question of Palestinian refugees. Christian ethics, while

---

[27] Reinhold Niebuhr, "Mission and Opportunity: Religion in 'Pluralistic Culture'," in *Social Responsibility in an Age of Revolution*, ed. Louis Finkelstein (New York: Jewish Theological Seminary of America, 1971).

relating its judgments to historical conditions, must not lose sight of the will of God that all people are to be granted conditions for the flowering of their humanity. Christian reflection favoring the security of Israel must also recognize Palestinian rights and insist that Israel deal more justly with Palestinians inside Israel and on the West Bank.[28]

---

[28] The part of this chapter beginning with "Christian Zionism" and following to the conclusion was published in another form as "The Zionism of Paul Tillich and Reinhold Niebuhr", *Tantur Yearbook 1980-81* (Jerusalem: Tantur, 1981), 219-33. A comparison of the two will show that this chapter stresses the early Zionism of Niebuhr more than did the previous paper. That correction is due to the helpful critique of Ursula Niebuhr and her calling to my attention certain sources from 1942. This paper was presented at the North American Paul Tillich Society meeting in Washington, D.C., November 19, 1993.

Chapter 4

ON THE BOUNDARY: PROTESTANTISM AND MARXISM[1]

Paul Tillich was born a Protestant, grew into a critical Marxist-Christian, and in the end fulfilled his life as a dominant Protestant theologian. He was born into that most Protestant of all social institutions: the pastor's family. Catholicism spurned the entanglement of family for its clergy and religious spiritual leaders. Eastern Orthodoxy relegated the family to second class status with its requirements that bishops be monks. Within Christianity, only Protestantism permitted and, until recently, in reality insisted, that its leadership be married clergymen. His early life and existence until World War I was patriarchal-Prussian-Lutheran existence as a pastor's son and pastor. He prepared in his education to follow in his father's footsteps in the learned-Brandenburg ministry.

---

[1] This chapter was presented at the North American Paul Tillich Society's Centenary celebration of the birth of Paul Tillich at Emory University in 1986, published in Mary Ann Stenger and Ronald H. Stone, *Dialogues of Paul Tillich* (Macon: Mercer University Press, 2002): 150-63, and revised for this volume.

Three artifacts I found symbolize the shocks that drove Tillich into his adult life-long conversation with Marxism. The first is from my Grandfather's attic in Humboldt, Iowa, and the second and third are from the Paul Tillich archives at Harvard.

As a young boy, it became necessary at my grandfather's death to clean out the family home. In the attic we found a German helmet from World War I, which had a crest reading *For Fatherland with God and King*. The helmet had been picked up on the Western front and its loss had probably cost some German-Christian soldier his head. I often remembered that helmet when I was working on the Paul Tillich papers in the Harvard Archives.

Tillich had left his boyhood home of dreaming innocence, his pastoral work in Berlin, and his patriarchal home with everything in place to go to war. He had his PhD in theology, he was married, and his family represented the learned German clergy. His father had served as chaplain to the Emperor on a trip to Jerusalem. It was a world of patriarchal capitalism, with the empire and Lutheranism in a symbiotic relationship. He went to war in a surge of patriotism and without clear political convictions. By the end of the war he had suffered nervous collapses repeatedly, he had helped bury the cream of the German office corps, his wife had become pregnant by his friend, and the empire had been defeated and thrown into revolution.

His first course in Berlin, "Christianity and the Social Problems of the Present," indicated the new social passions of the young Privatdozent. There are two cultural artifacts from this period in the Harvard Archives. The first is a flyer calling for a meeting to organize a new church. The program was summarized in four points:

(1) renew religious motifs in culture,
(2) support the new republic and socialism,
(3) align the church with the international peace movement,
(4) institute parliamentary control of the church.

The third is a red poster with a hammer and sickle symbol announcing that Paul Tillich will speak to a rally of Independent Social Democrats. Pastors Richard Wegener and Paul Tillich were called upon to justify their participation in the ISD rally. They wrote a paper for the Brandenburg consistory justifying their position. They argued:

(1) The personal encounter of the person and God is beyond any economic or social form,
(2) Christianity is inevitably involved with society,
(3) Christianity has greater affinity with socialism than with capitalism,
(4) Socialism had no essential fight with Christianity.

The reaction of the church hierarchy was hostile, and they were ordered not to speak at any more ISD rallies.

His socialism alienated him from the church of his father, but the socialism developed in small religious discussion groups. He understood his form of religious socialism not to be a movement for the whole church, but to be a small non-political movement which would reflect the development of the ideas rooted in social reality. Even as he led in various discussion circles he learned from others and depended on others for political-economic concepts. The groups lived on the boundary between socialism and religion.

Paul Tillich's special place on the boundary was the engagement of the early Karl Marx with Lutheranism. He could not stand the tendencies toward legalism and Biblicism that he found in Calvinism; the economics of *Das Kapital* and the determinist-scientific Marxist writers held little interest for him. But a trained economist with a passion for analyzing Calvinism influenced his methodological approach to the encounter with Marxist critique of bourgeois society.

THE USE OF MAX WEBER

Max Weber haunts the socialist writing of Paul Tillich. Basic concepts are taken over, utilized, and usually not acknowledged. I want to suggest that the importance of this is that Paul Tillich had already integrated Max Weber into his socialism by an early date. At least by 1926 the socialist presentation of Tillich was shaped by Weber. Weber had reshaped his own writing on religion and economics during the First World War, so the work was relatively fresh.

The central concept of *The Religious Situation* published in 1926 is "The Capitalist Spirit." It does not differ from Weber's concept "The Spirit of Capitalism." The explanation of the use of the term makes use of Weber's ideal type methodology. Tillich writes: "It is rather a symbol for an ultimate, fundamental attitude toward the world."[2] The purpose of the book is to show that the dominance of the spirit of capitalism is receiving significant challenges.

The economic organization of modernity arose on grounds of autonomy and the overthrow of superior powers. The economic influence dominates the selves that develop within the system. "The spirit of a finitude which lives within itself is, for our time, the spirit of capitalist society."[3] The awe and mystery of the world have been replaced by control of finite reality by humanity. Personality is freed from mystery and pressed into the bondage economic of living within a system of rational, calculating manipulation of reality. Economics comes to control life.

> This is one of the weightiest characteristics of the capitalist time. The goad of unlimited desire does not allow the spirit time for anything which does not serve time itself. It drives the spirit about within the inescapable and unending circle of the finite.[4]

---

[2] Paul Tillich, *The Religious Situation*, trans. H.R. Niebuhr (New York: Henry Holt and Company, 1932), xxv.

[3] Tillich, 71.

[4] Tillich, 75.

The personality of early twentieth century humanity is portrayed by Tillich as living in Max Weber's iron cage.

In 1926, Tillich had moved beyond the early romantic socialism of revolutionary enthusiasm. The book did not show the full movement into and transformation of socialist categories that the 1933 work *The Socialist Decision* would exhibit. The 1926 study is more a critique of the culture while hoping for a religious change. By 1933 he is proposing a program for changing society and resisting the Nazi coup.

The Religious Situation showed how completely sectarian Christianity and Calvinism had merged in North America with capitalism. They reinforced each other in a way which appeared impregnable to Tillich. Neither Catholicism nor Lutheranism revealed a social program fit to the crisis. In prophetic critique and pre-capitalist Catholic religiosity he saw some hope for a religious orientation against the capitalist spirit of "the ideal of a self-sufficient finitude."[5] He saw Protestantism bereft of an independent culture, so the resistance to capitalism will come from its greatest source of strength, its theological work. Still, *The Religious Situation* is basically an analysis of the way things are and from whence they have come, and it does not show the goals or power of transformation.

A few years later he explicitly referred to his use of these broad concepts as ideal types. The proletariat was described as a class dependent upon the sale of their labor under market conditions. He said the concept was not entirely an empirical concept but a representative or typological one.[6]

The next year he used the term *principal* "to refer to the summarizing characterization of a political group."[7] Principal was a way to avoid the endless empirical particularities and to refer to dynamics

---

[5] Tillich, 117.

[6] Paul Tillich, *Political Expectation.*

[7] Paul Tillich, *The Socialist Decision*, trans. Franklin Sherman (New York: Harper & Row Publishers, 1977), 9.

of a movement or to its spirit. It also emphasized the decision or existentialist character of identifying a group with its central powerful idea. So with the term principal he can carry forward the typological, descriptive-critical work of *The Socialist Decision*.

The utilization of Weber's method to describe Marxist ideas began to transform Marxism. Religion could never be only a byproduct of the substructure of the society. Economic materialism as taught by some Marxists is excluded by method from the system. Metaphysical materialism is overthrown by a descriptive method forged to demonstrate the relative significance of religious-intellectual phenomena. Historical materialism remains a possibility over against an historical idealism. Tillich affirms materialism but most of this affirmation is making use of unacknowledged Weberian ideal types. Furthermore, Marxism is a term used to describe the growing self-realization of the proletariat in overcoming their alienated situation. This equation of Marxism with this growing consciousness meant it was not primarily an idea but the power of a movement. It also meant that if the power faded so did Marxism.

THE SOCIALIST DECISION

In 1929, when he joined the Social Democratic Party, it was to strengthen the party now out of power for a return to power to oppose groups bearing other ideas. He tried to join religion and social democracy calling on both religion and social democracy to reform. Their separation and antagonism reflected the human estrangement. Their union would have given the possibility of a theonomous political movement.

The ideas of reform, planning, and criticism of social democracy were reinforced by ideas within Protestantism. Protestantism's reform and critique needed to be reinforced by myths of origin or catholicity, while socialism needed the principle of expectation which could be best grasped in religious terms. But neither enough Socialists nor enough Christians could be persuaded to join these historically antagonistic movements. He tried to unite conceptually those which historically were opposed.

The Socialist Decision is his most creative political philosophy. He wrote it under pressure. Two months after its publication he was suspended from his university position in Frankfurt. But it was not only inspired by the pressure, he had a program: the reform of socialism so that it could resist Nazism.

The volume expresses his deeply speculative mind as it organizes the fruit of fourteen years of socialist conversations and previous lectures. It also represents Tillich the fighter, who fought as a philosopher could best fight by criticizing Nazi claims to truth by explaining, criticizing, and relativizing Nazi thought. The hope for the success of his program rested in the variable of moving revolutionary support away from the political romanticism of Nazism to the critical politics of social democracy.

The introduction to the volume of two types of political philosophy was translated and published in English in *The Interpretation of History*. The remainder of the volume awaited Franklin Sherman's publication of a translation in 1977. The two types are those founded in myths of origin and those originating in prophetic criticism of those myths. Other political movements bearing political ideas can be analyzed fruitfully in terms of expansions of these concepts. Hence Nazism is analyzed as a revolutionary form of political romanticism as it attacks the present in terms of a radical reading of myths of origin, i.e., blood, soil, nation. The spirit of Judaism rooted in prophetic criticism is essentially opposed to political romanticism.

Other sections of the book move beyond the analysis of political romanticism to analyze Western capitalism as akin to Western socialism in sharing the critique of the myths of origin. Western capitalism's progressivism depended upon the myth of harmony, i.e., "the invisible hand" of Adam Smith, and that myth too is dissolved in socialist criticism.

Socialism is criticized for its unresolved problems as socialist hopes seemed to outrun socialist possibilities. Socialism reflected the powers of origin in the realities of the anguish of its proletarian population. It criticized the belief in harmony, and it demanded change. The demand for change remained heteronomous without the concept of *expectation.* Expectation, the worldly eschatology of prophetic religion, is necessary if the tensions of socialism are to be resolved. It is the prophetic expectation that the new can emerge. Expectation indicates that the demands of ethics of critical consciousness are supported by the powers of origin. Hence there is hope. There may be chaos and barbarism, but the powers of change reflect the powers of origin, so they can be trusted. The religious roots of socialism are seen in this concept of expectation. Despite his valiant tries in the volume to avoid utopianism, the sense of expectation that religious people and socialists could ally in 1933 in a political movement seems utopian. He saw the possibility of defeat and he could predict, and he did predict, barbarism, war, and chaos if political romanticism prevailed.

Shortly before the Nazi electoral gains he had a dream of sheep grazing in the deserted yards of the center of government in Berlin's Potzdammer Platz. After the war he saw in a New York newspaper a picture of sheep grazing in Potzdammer Platz. It is only a short walk from the buildings of the "Thousand Year Reich" to the Kaiser Wilhelm Memorial Church. Here the ruined remains of imperial Germany are united in their bombed-out form with the new church structure. I like to think that this was the church where in 1933 Hannah had to restrain Paul's curses and obscene gestures when they exited from a Nazi-dominated church meeting. Cursing the sick culture and prostituted church of Germany in 1933 was appropriate. Heinrich Heine, a Jew, prophesied correctly that the cathedrals were doomed.

> Christianity—and this is its fairest merit—subdued to a certain extent the brutal warrior ardour of the Germans, but it could not entirely quench it; and when the cross, that restraining talisman, falls

> to pieces, then will break forth again the ferocity of the old combatants, the frantic Berserker rage whereof Northern poets have said and sung so much. The talisman has become rotten, and the day will come when it will pitifully crumble to dust. The old stone gods will arise then from the forgotten ruins and wipe from their eyes the dust of centuries, and Thor with his giant hammer will arise again, and he will shatter the Gothic cathedrals.[8]

CONCEPT OF HUMANITY

In 1935, Tillich wrote a report on "The Christian and the Marxist View of Man" for the Universal Christian Council for Life and Work Research Department.9 It continues the anthropological explorations that were present in *The Socialist Decision* and makes the analogies between his Protestantism and Marxism quite clear. Part of the report is still in outline form and many of the sources of Tillich's thought are referred to only by name and their specific contributions left undeveloped. A second edition of the paper was developed in 1959 and that version of the paper is extant in the Harvard Archive. The report is complete enough to be a prospectus for a major study, perhaps a small book. It is not surprising that he was still engaged at a deep level with Marxism in 1959. He continued publishing on Marxism in the United States through the 30s, 40s, and 50s and in Germany and Japan in 1960. The evidence of the works of Tillich is contrary to the assertion by Walter Weisskopf in *The Thought of Paul Tillich* that "Tillich's socialist writings stem from the time before his emigration to the US and therefore does not cover

---

[8] Quoted in Beate von Oppen, *Religion and Resistance to Nazism* (Princeton: Princeton University Center of International Studies, 1971), 9.

[9] Paul Tillich, "The Christian and the Marxist View of Man," 1935 and 1959, unpublished typescript, Paul Tillich Papers, Andover-Harvard Theological Library, Cambridge.

events after 1933."[10] The report, outline, prospectus, or essay, is a reminder that the life-long, primary-dialogue partner to Paul Tillich's Protestantism was Marxism. John Stumme has dated the origins of this dialogue with Marxism to work with the proletariat and a debate on December 12, 1913 with Karl Liebknecht who later organized the German Communist Party.11

The first section of the paper shows that neither Marxism nor some tendencies in Protestantism have an "articulate anthropology." Their refusal to articulate anthropology in both cases was rooted in their negative evaluation of historical existence. However, within both Protestantism and Marxism developments have produced anthropologies which try to unite radically critical attitudes with anthropology capable of supporting hope for healing. Their convergent trends reveal their common prophetic heritage and make comparisons possible. The second section of the paper is an outline presentation of the basic ideas of Protestant anthropology. The result of the presentation is to show that there are six problems of equal importance to Christianity and Marxism: humanity's original true nature, the transition to a state of contradiction, the character of this contradiction, existence in contradiction, the overcoming of the contradiction, and the goal of the perfection of humanity.[12]

The exploration of the six problems in the third section demonstrates that there are structural analogies between prophetic Christianity and Marxism, especially in its original form in Marx himself. He does not intend to argue for identity of ideas but to show typologically certain analogies. As the second section had begun "The galvanizing point of view of Christian-Protestant anthropology is

---

[10] Walter Weisskopf, "Tillich and the Crisis of the West," in *The Thought of Paul Tillich*, eds. James L. Adams, Wilhelm Pauck, Roger L. Shinn (San Francisco, Harper & Row Publishers, 1985), 76

[11] John R. Stumme, *Socialism in Theological Perspective* (Missoula: Scholars Press, 1978), 55.

[12] Tillich, "The Christian View of Man," 5.

the relation of man to God," the third section begins: "The controlling viewpoint of all socialist-Marxist anthropology is man's position within society."[13] Then the analogies in the six areas are presented.

The fourth and final section of the paper shows the contradictions between Christianity and Marxism in the areas where structural analogies were found. In each case the fundamental antithesis is one of immanence and transcendence. Christian anthropology is related to God and Marxist anthropology to society. All of the fundamental oppositions can be seen to be an expression of the transcendence-immanence issue.

Marxism is seen as adopting one element, that of the critical-prophetic motif, while Christianity also preserves the possibilities of mysticism and a certain inward existence distinct from social contradictions. Conditions of the relationship between Marxism and Christianity depend on whether the relationship is exclusive or particular; the first possibility of interpretation leads to life-and-death struggle. The second interpretation, which was that of religious socialism, would understand Marxism as the critical-prophetic-immanent tendency of Christianity's own life. Such an interpretation would then regard it as the task of the church to "search for a way of receiving it again into itself." This tightly outlined and argued paper then ends with this plea for reunion of the separated and the return of the prophetic elements to their religious roots.

NEAR THE END

The existentialist's notes become louder in his 1960 essay, "On the Boundary," published for *The Christian Century* in the "How My Mind Has Changed." He admits the reasons for his lessened political interest.[14] It was a time of prevailing trends and not of decisive

[13] Tillich, 5, 9.

[14] Paul Tillich, "How My Mind Has Changed," *The Christian Century* 77 (December 7, 1960): 1435-37.

actions. Political decisions were confined to small power groups which excluded wide general influence on significant decisions. The neurotic conditions of the world were seen in neurotic individuals. As a German-born American it wasn't a time for his own expressions of German religious-socialism. He did not really understand American politics, etc. But then, as always, his work was in response to requests. Harvard asked him to lecture on German philosophy and on religion and culture. Not many were asking for fresh work on religious socialism in the United States. Tillich of course was never a pure existentialist. Those years at Harvard saw the essentialism emphasized in Volume III and in the Harvard courses. However, the existentialism appeared in the focus on the individual.

Here, the Lutheranism emerges dominant. He had always known of the more radical place for the individual in Christian faith, but in these final years it becomes dominant in his preaching and particularly in his emphasis on psychology and mental health. In 1935 he had written:

> The transcendential foundation offers Christianity the possibility of disassociating to a certain existence the inward existence of the individual from among the structural framework of the objective contradiction. This is the ground of the possibility of the care of individual souls and of mysticism within Christianity. In Marxism, however, such a disengagement of the interior existence of the individual is made impossible by the purely social interpretation of the contradiction.[15]

By 1960 this possibility of the care of individual souls had become dominant in his work. He now tended to lecture on religion and society and not often on religious socialism. He rooted his social action in fighting the demonic, not in the expectation of victory in society.

John Stumme has summarized the approach of his closing years

---

[15] Tillich, "The Christian View of Man,"16.

well. "There was for him no going 'beyond religious socialism.'"[16] Religious socialism had been his venture from the end of World War I to the end of World War II; pragmatic, reform politics were in order after World War II. The church had to wait passionately and actively for signs of a new theonomy. The doctrine of the *kairos*, even if sometimes romantic, had always meant there were periods without the *kairos*.

During the spring quarter of 1962-63 at the Divinity School of the University of Chicago, Tillich made a remark in his lectures on the history of Christian thought on the importance of Karl Marx. The remark needs to be taken seriously as a clue to the importance of Marx for his ongoing thought.

> What I will do now is perhaps surprising to you. I want to give you here the theology of the most successful of all theologians since the Reformation, namely, Karl Marx. I will consider him as a theologian. And I will show you that without doing this, it is impossible to understand the history of the twentieth century and large sections of the late nineteenth century. If you consider him only as a political leader or as a great economist, who he also was, or as a great sociologist, which he was even more, then you cannot understand from what sources the power came which transformed the whole world and conquered nearly half of it in the twentieth century.[17]

STAGES OF SOCIALISM

Appropriate political action always accounts for the cultural possibilities. To act without recognizing the cultural limits is utopian. Politics for Tillich, however, is not just adjusting to culture; it may mean opposition to the dominant culture. The drive to oppose culture arises from ethics and the ability to discern possibilities for change.

---

[16] Stumme, *Socialism,* 255.

[17] Paul Tillich, *A History of Christian Thought*, ed. Carl E. Braaten (New York: Simon and Schuster, 1968), 476.

Ethics is the understanding of practical activity toward the realization of the Unconditioned. Ethics won't realize the ideal community, but by expressing action guides in transcendent symbols it affects the community's action. Despite the complexity of the biographical formulation of Tillich's ethic and the wide range of sources from which it is drawn, the form of this ethic is clear and consistent.

The structure is threefold: first, the ultimate principle of Christian ethics is *agape* which is known as the law of human nature; second, human wisdom is represented in laws, moral principles, guidelines; third, the concrete situation in which the actor takes upon himself the risk of moral decision. This pattern of love, law, and situation is present in most of Tillich's writing on ethics.

Agape is the one universal element of the human moral situation. Occasionally, he describes the universal element as "the human self." The seeming ambivalence in his ethics, of course, derives from his claim that a properly conducted analysis of human nature reveals love as the essence of life. Though in much of his writing it would rather seem that the experience of love is the starting point of the analysis: "In man's experience of love the nature of life becomes manifest."[18]

The second level of the theory accepts the relativity of all moral principles unless they are alternative formulations of *agape*, which in itself includes justice and the honoring of a person as a person. Moral principles or middle axioms are not despised, but they are thoroughly relativized. They are useful as guidelines. If they are embodied *agape* and if they meet the situation, they are that which the moral decision maker acts upon.

The third level requires loving listening. It is at this level that the tools of the social and psychological sciences have their most importance for Tillich. His anti-moralism demands that as many of

---

[18] Paul Tillich, *Love, Power, and Justice* (New York: Oxford University Press, 1954), 25.

the particulars of the situation are understood as possible. There is no security, but only the risk of moral decision and the comfort that trust in the power of forgiveness gives.

Love as the absolute is the principle of justice which keeps it creative. Justice forms the society in a relationship which allows development of human beings in community. Being under conditions of human life can express itself in a form encouraging unity and growth.

It seemed to Tillich in 1919 that religious socialism expressed the absolute, was appropriate to the principles of human wisdom, and was the decision to be made. I think that by 1932 religious socialism was a less direct expression of the absolute, but it was still an appropriate action to be taken even at the risk of career and life, as it expressed the best human option. By 1965 it seems that religious socialism was no longer an expression of the absolute for many societies, it was still for him the best human option available, and it could not find a place in the American soil to flourish.

Marxism had remained a dialogue partner of Tillich's from the German revolution after World War I until his death in 1965. His lecture on Karl Marx in the academic year 1962-1963 at the University of Chicago repeated what he himself found of enduring value in the thought of Karl Marx.

(1) Historical materialism. After Marx, it was no longer possible to think of isolated individuals who were independent of society. Human life was dependent upon the social-economic realities.

(2) Alienation. The Marxist theories of society contributed to human understanding the thesis that in historical life all human existence is estranged from its true meaning and that its creations reflect and continue this estrangement.

(3) Ideology. Marxist analysis revealed how ideas and, particularly important for Tillich, religions and philosophic ideas could reflect false consciousness as they justified or protected unfair aspects of human relations. Much of religion did actually reflect the self-

interests of the dominant classes.

(4) Critique of religion. Marxist critique revealed the church's need for self-correction and the overcoming of the estrangement between the working classes and the religious establishment.

For Tillich, the Marxist critique failed and turned into totalitarianism because it rejected God and lost principles of internal critique. The group of the vanguard or remnant itself became self-righteous and blind to its own idolatrous ideology because it suppressed the reference to the Ultimate.[19] So for Tillich, Marxist atheism defeated itself. Religious socialism which could have preserved the best of social reform and social revolution was too sophisticated. The masses would support religion or socialism, but not the required synthesis. The dialogue of Protestantism and Marxism occupied his mind, but the social reality eluded him.

[19] Tillich, *A History of Christian Thought*, 476-87.

Chapter 5

RESISTANCE TO THE THIRD REICH[1]

World Wars I and II called him to participate, and while I interpret him as a theologian of peace, he was also a theologian of war. War came upon him with irresistible force and though he would act as a philosopher of war, he knew also of the weapons of war, particularly, the ideological weapons.

A major motif of Tillich's thought about war is found in his various writings on war aims. War aims correspond closely to one of the points of just war theory: the goal of a war must be just. Tillich chose to organize much of his thought about war around this teleological point. What are the appropriate aims of the war? The aims

---

[1] Much of this chapter was published as "The Aims of World War II," in Mary Ann Stenger and Ronald H. Stone, *Dialogues of Paul Tillich* (Macon: Mercer University Press, 2002), 222-40. This chapter also utilizes edited pages from Ronald H. Stone, *Paul Tillich's Radical Social Thought* (Atlanta: John Knox Press, 1980); Ronald H. Stone, ed., *Theology of Peace* (Louisville: Westminster John Knox, 1990); Ronald H. Stone and Matthew Lon Weaver, eds., *Against the Third Reich* (Louisville: Westminster/John Knox Press, 1998); and pages original to this chapter.

of the war would then assist in organizing the way the war should be fought and strategies chosen.

There are five major locations for his discussion of war aims. His articles on war aims in *The Protestant Digest*, his papers for the Federal Council of Churches Commission on a Just and Durable Peace, his statement of purpose for the Council for a Democratic Germany, his speeches to German listeners in Europe from March 1942 to May 1944, and his essay "the World Situation" are the major sources for these discussions of aims. The five contexts affect the presentations of the goals of the war, but all five portray a consistency. All five contexts reflect his urging warfare upon armies in which relatives served his own beloved homeland, his universities, and the culture for which he had fought thirty years earlier.

THE COMING OF WAR

The closing months of 1938 and the spring and summer of 1939 were busy months of international diplomacy. The democracies of France and England vacillated before the determined, aggressive diplomacy of Italy, Japan, and Germany. The United States remained ineffective, and the Soviet Union contemplated various security arrangements that would further its interests. In retrospect, it was a time of deciding when the war would come and who would be allies.

Located between the major powers, the weaker countries including Finland, Estonia, Latvia, Lithuania, Poland, and Czechoslovakia were the bargaining chips of the deadly game being played. Earlier appeasement in the Far East, Africa, and Spain had encouraged the fascists to risk belligerency.

The Munich pact of September 1938 sacrificed Czechoslovakia to Hitler and encouraged Stalin to divide Poland with Hitler the following summer. The French and English bought peace in Munich, and Russia bought peace from Ribbentrop in Moscow in August 1939. The two pacts for peace insured that war would come. Tillich knew that no compromise was possible with Nazism. In

1938, aware of the relativities of judgment and ambiguity of political action, he had called for a life-and-death struggle against Nazism.[2]

Commenting on the Munich agreement before the outbreak of war, Tillich isolated five factors as presuppositions of the situation: those people operating in nineteenth century categories of continual progress were unprepared to understand events of the twentieth century; the foreign policies of the various countries depended upon the interests of the ruling classes; the politics of leftist forces in the democracies were inept; fascism promised an answer to the insecurities of the present; collective security had not worked, and the Munich settlement recognizing a German protectorate over central Europe was unstable.[3]

War seemed inevitable. The encirclement policy that followed Munich was a reaction of the old empires to the new German empire. The policy depended upon Russia, and Tillich feared that dependence on Russia was foolhardy.

Several contradictory conditions in Germany were obvious to Tillich. There was a contradiction between the mass movement of Nazism and its foundation of terror. Capitalism was being both preserved and transformed. Economic problems were being resolved by a war economy, but the economy was threatened by a war conducted by a mass society. The rhetoric was of both nationalism and supranational imperialism. All these instabilities in Germany were overcome by repression.

Tillich thought in 1939 that there was still a chance that the emergence of a German empire in central Europe would be tolerated by the democracies. However, if Germany reached agreement with Russia, war would follow. He recognized that the Russian-German

---

[2] Paul Tillich, "The Gospel and the State," *Crozer Quarterly* 15, no. 4 (1938): 241-61.

[3] Paul Tillich, "The Political Situation in Europe," unpublished typescript, Paul Tillich Papers, Andover-Harvard Theological Library, Cambridge.

alliance must be prevented, but that it was probably too late to stop it, and he supported the growing toughness of Roosevelt's foreign policy.

Religious leadership, he felt, had been largely irresponsible in the face of the developing situation. In a short discussion of power and justice, he refuted religious pacifism as a possible response. In order for Democracy to survive it would have to realize internal justice and not just observe the forms of legal justice. In the twentieth century, the emptiness of meaning and the lack of justice allowed demonic totalitarianism to rush into the vacuum.

The German invasion of Poland on September 1, 1939, with the assistance of Russia, drove Tillich into a period of discouragement and despair. He had anticipated war and urged preparation for it, but the actuality of it brought back too many painful dreams and memories of his own time in the trenches of World War I. During this second world conflagration his actions were first to become an American citizen and then to join in the public debate over the aims and policies of the war, to continue to assist refugees, to write on the war, and to join the American propaganda war after the United States was brought into the conflict.

Tillich's work among refugees had emphasized the need for a real migration. He urged Germans to identify with their new country and to free themselves from illusory hopes for a return. On March 4, 1940 he became a US citizen, and in an essay celebrating his new status, he affirmed his ability as a citizen to participate in building the future.[4] Europe, for him, became identified more and more with the past.

---

[4] Paul Tillich, "I Am an American," *Protestant Digest* 2, no. 4 (June-July 1941): 24-26. See also "The Conquest of Theological Provincialism," in *The Cultural Migration: The European Scholar in America*, ed. Franz L. Neumann, et al. (Philadelphia: University of Pennsylvania Press, 1953), 138-56.

THE PROTESTANT

In 1941, Kenneth Leslie attracted Tillich to his journal *The Protestant Digest* (soon changed to *The Protestant*), and Tillich wrote several essays for it in 1941-43. Leslie was a rather independent editor, and he was constantly in tension with his editorial board, of which Paul Tillich became chairman. One of the disputes led Tillich to write a policy statement for the journal in 1942. It is one of Tillich's most succinct statements of the relationship of Christian faith to political action; it appeared under the title "Protestant Principles."[5]

> (1) Protestantism affirms the absolute majesty of God alone and raises prophetic protest against every human claim, ecclesiastical or secular, to absolute truth and authority.
>
> (2) Protestantism affirms the Christian message as the ultimate expression of the nature of the Divine and protests against all attempts to dissolve this message into a complex of religious experiences, moral demands and philosophical doctrines.
>
> (3) Protestantism affirms Divine sovereignty over the institutions and doctrines of the Christian churches and protests against attempts to bind the Christian message to the life and law of any historical church.
>
> (4) Protestantism affirms the direct reference of the Divine to every element of reality and protests against hierarchical meditations as well as against the separation of a sacred from a secular realm.
>
> (5) Protestantism affirms the independent structure of the different spheres of the cultural life and protests against encroachments upon their autonomy by churches and states.
>
> (6) Protestantism affirms the dependence of the spiritual meaning of all cultural activities on their religious foundation and protests

[5] Paul Tillich, "Protestant Principles," *The Protestant* 4, no. 5 (April-May 1942), 17.

against the separation of religious transcendence from cultural immanence.

(7) Protestantism, while rejecting any definitive or final system of Christian ethics and politics, applies the Christian message to every historical situation as the principle of criticism and demand.

In a following issue of the journal Tillich commented on the principles in response to readers' reactions.[6] He set out his belief that the essence of Protestantism or prophetic religion is the dual recognition of the transcendence and immanence of God. All of life had a religious base, but life itself is not divine. Religion has two senses: its special proclamation of its vision of God and the denial that its special proclamation is absolute. All of life points toward its source, but the source is not captured by any expression of life. Vital religion announces the "end of religion" in the sense of criticizing the absolute pretensions of religious communities, but vital religion continues to affirm the human need for religious symbols to express the ultimate.

This dialectical approach conditions Protestantism's relationship to both the church and the world. Both are affirmed, both are criticized. Therefore, in politics there is no absolute Christian answer, but continual Christian engagement in the pursuit of answers. "Protestantism is not bound to its past; therefore it is free for its future, even if this future should deserve the name 'Post Protestant Era.'"[7]

Tillich's first statement regarding appropriate war aims had appeared in 1941 in *The Protestant Digest*. He blamed the democracies for creating communism by nurturing social injustice and of having used fascism to combat communism. The war was a struggle by fascism to destroy the humanism of the West, he argued, and the appropriate war aim should be the creation of a planned economy in a

---

[6] Paul Tillich, *The Protestant* 4, no. 7 (August-September 1941), 8-14.
[7] Tillich, 14.

European federal union, which could be liberal enough to prevent tyranny while assuring economic security to the masses of Europe. Liberal arbitrariness could be overcome without sacrificing freedom, he thought, and nationalism reduced by an economic federation. The war aims that appeared in serial form in the journal were brought together as a pamphlet and sold for a nickel to contribute to the American discussion of goals of the war.[8]

Eventually the sponsors of the journal differed over the editorial position regarding communism. *The Protestant* folded as a result of the dispute, and Leslie, who was too close to communism for many on the board, returned to his native Canada. The split among the sponsors of the journal was symptomatic of what happened to many of Tillich's projects in the war period, and beyond that, foreshadowed the tensions that would divide the victors of World War II and result in the Cold War.

AGAINST THE THIRD REICH

Paul Tillich prepared 112 five-page addresses in German for broadcast into occupied Europe from March 1942 through May 1944. Even his closest friends in the USA did not know of his secret work for the Allied cause. These addresses have been largely unknown in the USA except for specialists in Tillich scholarship. The essays in *Against the Third Reich* are among the most concrete and passionate of his political writings. They also show that this Protestant theologian who could announce the end of the Protestant era and castigate Protestantism so thoroughly was also a German Protestant theologian who saw the demonic, named it, and did what he could as a theologian to denounce it. The reader of these essays will learn that Tillich's analysis was not only profound, powerful, and polemical, but that it was also true. These radio speeches are the raw data of a theologian at war from 1942-1944, following the daily events and

[8] Paul Tillich, *War Aims* (New York: Protestant Digest, 1941).

analyzing them theologically. These are not works from hindsight, but engaged, political-theological risk taking.[9]

Tillich's writing began at an Allied low point in the war, moved through the Axis defeats of 1942, and concluded before D-Day in mid-1944. Throughout this period, Tillich optimistically trusted in the ultimate Allied victory. The United States and the Soviet Union were both stronger than Germany. With the empire to draw upon, Britain's strength was certainly as great as Japan's, and the lesser nations of the world were drawn into functional alliances with the Allies. Tillich regarded the outcome as certain, but one to be achieved through much suffering and hard fighting. In terms of population and industrial production, the Allies were too strong for the Axis powers. The military skills of the democrats and the communists were to be proven as in no way inferior to those of the Nazis, Fascists, and Japanese militarists. Tillich portrayed Hitler as a gambler who had taken a contest at bad odds. Having lost his gamble, Hitler compulsively tried to repair his losses, but when defeated, his actions turned into an orgy of German self-destruction. Should we regard Tillich as too optimistic? Probably not, most Americans of Tillich's generation with whom we've spoken also regarded the outcome of the war as a foregone conclusion. After all, Pittsburgh itself would outproduce the Ruhr Valley. Once US production was geared up, more aircraft and ships would flow from North American mills on the invulnerable continent than the Japanese could destroy. Tillich's judgments were shrewd, formulated from experience in the trenches of World War I. It is worth remembering that his rank in World

[9] Ronald H. Stone and Matthew Lon Weaver, eds., *Against the Third Reich: Paul Tillich's Wartime Radio Broadcasts into Nazi Germany* (Louisville: Westminster/John Knox Press, 1998). References to Tillich's transcripts give their date, and they have been translated from the German by Matthew Lon Weaver in *Against the Third Reich.* The original German transcripts can be found in the Paul Tillich Papers of the Andover-Harvard Theological Library, Cambridge.

War I was higher than either Hitler's or Eisenhower's. By the time of his writing, Hitler and Japan's mistakes had doomed their regimes. Hitler's "Barbarosa" invasion of the Soviet Union perhaps had a chance in 1941 if Japan had struck the USSR in the East. But Japan's foolish attack on the USA and Hitler's declaration of war on the world's strongest industrial power sealed their fate. If Stalin, in the sure knowledge that Japan was committed elsewhere, had not been able to shift 32 divisions from the East to thwart the Nazis at the gates of Moscow in the first winter, things might have been different. But by March of 1942, Tillich could see the Nazi defeat. The turning points came in North Africa in 1942 and at Stalingrad in early 1943 for Germany. In addition to population, material, and military intelligence, will was needed to defeat the Axis. Both Japan and Germany in their terrible barbaric excesses aroused in communists and democrats the will to fight.

Tillich for his part was trying to divide the will of his German listeners from the mania of its Nazi rulers. Again and again he hit the theme Nazism is doomed, abandon it. He tried to persuade Germans to stop cooperating with their rulers. This attempt, of course, confronted the obedient character of the good German. Just by listening to his broadcasts, a German or other European was engaging in resistance. A Czech theologian put it to me: "The broadcasts of the Voice of America were very important to us, but we could be executed for listening."

His first speech to "My German Friends"—as Tillich began each of the "Voice of America" talks—was against anti-Semitism. It was logical for Tillich to begin his speeches with "the Jewish question," both existentially and intellectually. Nazi atrocities against Jews had begun prior to his exit from Germany in the early 1930s.[10] They were a fact of life that had to be confronted. Further, the

[10] Wilhelm Pauck and Marion Pauck, *Paul Tillich: His Life and Thought* (San Francisco: Harper & Row Publishers, 1976), 127-30.

historic identity of the Jewish people had a significant place in his theology as well as his philosophy of history. Theologically, they are the inspiration for his notion of the Protestant principle, that element of perpetual critique which stands against the ever-present threats of idolatry and utopianism.[11] Historically, Jewish prophetism is the vehicle for his argument of the dominance of time over space as the necessary prerequisite for the existence of justice.[12] Tillich began his speeches at this point because "the Jewish question" was central to his thought. Before 1942 was over, Tillich was writing of the Nazi actions of extermination of the Jews (September 12, 1942 and November 12, 1942). In December of that year he was telling Germans of the trains of death, of the machine gun executions of Jewish children and women, and of German physicians who joined in the slaughter in the camps. The Nazi guilt was a burden to the country that had become the tool for Nazism. So these essays move on from March 1942 to May 1944, detailing the guilt of all responsible Germans. Types and degrees of guilt can be distinguished, but Germany's guilt is detailed, and Tillich's own guilt fuels the passion of his writing. He does not ignore guilt for the breakdown of German democracy attributable to the other nations. But his focus on the guilt for the horror of the war, the extermination campaigns, and the assault against humanity is on Germans. The faults in Germany are deep and he expounds on German character, myth, and history, but responsibility rests upon those who allowed Hitler to enslave them. The majority of the addresses urge Germans to act to liberate

---

[11] Paul Tillich, "The Protestant Principle and the Proletarian Situation," in *the Protestant Era* (Chicago: The University of Chicago Press, 1948), 161-81.

[12] Paul Tillich, "The Struggle between Space and Time," in *Theology and Culture* (London: Oxford University Press, 1959), 31, 32; and Paul Tillich, *The Socialist Decision* (New York: Harper & Row Publishers, 1977; reprinted Washington, D.C.: The University Press of America, 1982), 6, 20, 22. Citations refer to the University Press of America edition.

themselves from the Nazis. But historically the Germans could not liberate themselves, and the Russians had to bear the brunt of that liberation struggle. But though Russian Communism brought liberation from Nazism, it also brought a new tyranny to millions of Germans. The united, cooperative Germany that Tillich hoped for after the liberation had to wait until the 1990s.

The addresses are theology of culture. The culture is terribly evil, and though many are guilty, the Nazis utilizing the Germans are particularly guilty. Redemption could come if the Germans could liberate themselves, but it becomes apparent that they cannot. In fact, as the war closes in on its climax, the conquest of Germany by the Allies promises only a partial liberation. Tillich's own political leadership in the German émigré organization, the Council for a Democratic Germany, falters on the clash between democrats and communists who will divide and oppress much of Germany. World War II was for Tillich a war to liberate Europe and Germany from the Nazis. The results of the war of liberation turn out, as they almost always do, very ambiguously. It is a theology for very troubled nations upon whom judgment has come or is coming in its historically ambiguous character. The hope for self-liberation is recognized by the author but not historically realized. Judgment and retribution against evil are more certain in this theology than liberation. Also, the question of Israel's salvation is close to the center of the story. Can poor Israel, crushed beneath the superpower, be liberated? For Tillich, by 1942, not much of European Israel would be saved, but a remnant for a restored home in Palestine was a hope. He compared the forthcoming destruction of Germany to the Biblical plagues suffered by Egypt for the slavery and liberation of Israel.

In one of his last addresses chosen for this volume, "One Hundred Speeches on Liberation from Nazism" (March 7, 1944), Tillich tells his listeners he has tried to encourage them to separate from Nazism. He affirms he speaks for Germany to find liberation from Nazism or, in a cautionary note, at least from the spirit of Nazism.

Expression of support for Germany while opposing Nazism would not be easily understood by American bureaucrats. Before the war ended Tillich would be blacklisted by the US Army as pro-German. He was deeply pro-German and very deeply pro-Jewish and totally anti-Nazi.

WAR AIMS IN THE SPEECHES

In the speeches more than in his other writings, the war becomes a struggle to destroy Nazism. It is seen as a war of Christian culture against evil. It is to be conducted with a holy passion against the evil of Nazism without hatred for the Nazis as persons (September 12, 1942). The war was waged, he assured his German listeners, to liberate Germany from the Nazis (October 6, 1942). In addition to the breaking of the death machine of Nazism, the war criminals must be punished. For him this is the doing of justice. It is to punish crimes against humanity. It will be a worldwide judgment against their crimes, and he argued there would be no refuge in the whole world for their crimes against humanity. He returns to the need to punish the Nazis so often that it must be recognized as a war aim for him. "It is the response of that which is divine in the world to the attempt to distort it into that which is diabolical" (October 20, 1942).

Repeatedly he describes the Germans as enslaved, and he calls for them to act against their enslavers. Victory in the war can mean freedom for Germans as well as their victims. Freedom for the allies was also a war aim and for Tillich it meant not only constitutional rights but the fulfillment of personal security in a fairer society represented by Roosevelt's domestic policies.

Another war aim articulated in the speeches is for the restoration of community among European nations and in the world. Technology and war have revealed the world to be one. Nazism violated the developing world community, and the goal of the war is to restore that community with a de-Nazified Germany having a place in the unity of nations. In the speech of July 17, 1942, Tillich identified himself with the progressives speaking of regional and world federations which would deny to the nations the rights or capacities to make war. He affirmed the developing plans for a stronger world organization than the previous League of Nations.

In summary, the speeches are less specific, considering their length, than the other sources on war aims. The first theme of the speeches is Germans, liberate your selves from the Nazis. In the fervor of this goal, Tillich declares a war that is of the crusade form, but he does not use the term. Other goals are the freedom of the nations of the world, European internal security, and social-economic security.

A JUST AND DURABLE PEACE

One of the most creative responses of organized American Protestantism to the war was the work of the Federal Council of Churches' Commission on a Just and Durable Peace. Under the chairmanship of John Foster Dulles, the commission developed a philosophy of international relations and sponsored educational work in the churches on this complex subject. Dulles' moralism and his natural tendency as a lawyer toward legalism pervaded the commission's philosophy. The program of the commission was a program of those who expected to be victors in the war and who wanted to assume the responsibilities of power in creating a new order. It was very effective in lobbying for the replacement of the League of Nations with a stronger organization that would become the United Nations.

The commission knew when it invited Tillich to deliver a series of lectures that his perspective of German religious socialism would be different. However, the gap between the commission's inclination toward a Calvinist legalism and the Lutheran theologian's dynamism was greater than Dulles anticipated. Tillich delivered three addresses.[13] The content of the lectures is the main theme of the next chapter.

COUNCIL FOR A DEMOCRATIC GERMANY

Paul Tillich served as chairman of the Council for a Democratic Germany, a group of anti-Nazi German refugees. The council published its founding philosophy, "A Program for a Democratic Germany," in *Christianity and Crisis* in May of 1944, just before the D-Day invasion of June 6.[14] Though no author's name appears, the document was written by Tillich and represents political thought identical to that expressed elsewhere under his own name. Signers of the declaration included professors, ministers, businesspeople, politicians, actors, and writers, many of whose names are well known today. Also among the signers were those who had contact with the German underground resistance. American supporters of the statement included John C. Bennett, Norman Cousins, John Dewey, Harry Emerson Fosdick, Rufus M. Jones, Reinhold Niebuhr, William Scarlett, Dorothy Thompson, and Jonah B. Wise.

The statement presupposed that cooperation between the West and Russia was a necessary precondition for the reconstruction of Europe. Many of the signers, including the author, however, knew that such cooperation was only a precarious possibility. There were four major emphases.

Germany was part of the European problem. The defeat of Nazism and the liquidation of the Nazis were prerequisites to any solution of the problem. Also, those who supported the Nazis had to be deprived of political power. Though it assumed a disarmed

---

[13] Paul Tillich, "Christian Principles and Political Reality," "The Social Problem of a Just and Durable Peace," and "The International Problem of a Just and Durable Peace," in *Theology of Peace*, ed. Ronald Stone (Louisville: Westminster John Knox Press, 1990).

[14] "A Program for a Democratic Germany," *Christianity and Crisis* (May 15, 1944), 3-5.

Germany, the statement warned against a dismembered Germany, fearing irredentism.

The economic power of Germany should be conserved to avoid widespread poverty and future unrest. The German economic system had to be integrated with the rest of Europe to reduce the danger of German economic hegemony and rearmament.

The democratic forces in Germany must be allowed to assert themselves and encouraged to carry out the program of denazification. The vestiges of Nazism had to be expurgated from all aspects of life by the Germans themselves.

The education of the German people had to be carried out by Germans in a context that provided security and democracy. Nazism and its spurious idea of Germany must be removed from schools, universities, books, libraries, and other cultural media. Historical experience was the primary teacher, and the imposition of American education on Germans, particularly in the absence of social justice, would be folly. The document pleaded, as Tillich emphasized everywhere, for Americans to recognize and nurture healthy elements in German society so that the evil elements could be removed without creating a vacuum into which new evil forces would move.

The brief life of the council, 1944-1945, was characterized by internal divisions, and the refugees were unable to agree upon policy for postwar Germany. The council's basic opposition to extreme measures of punishment for Germany was criticized, and for a short time, Tillich was blacklisted by the US Army. Eventually, the tensions represented in the developing Cold War drained the council of its life, and it expired. What policy it had depended on a united Germany and some cooperation between the US and the USSR. With division and antagonism, it had no program. In later years when Tillich would refuse to participate in some political activities, he would point to his chairmanship of the council and attribute his withdrawal from active politics to its failure.

"THE WORLD SITUATION"

Since 1934 Tillich had met semiannually with a body that called itself the Theological Discussion Group. The gathering included the Niebuhr brothers, Roland Bainton, Robert Calhoun, John Bennett, Henry P. Van Dusen, Douglas Steere, George F. Thomas, John Mackay, Georgia Harkness, Benjamin Mays, John Knox, Theodore M. Greene, Samuel McCrea Cavert, Edwin E. Aubrey, Wilhelm Pauck, and others. Originally a young gathering, the group gradually came to represent something of an establishment in American theology. Its members considered the group an important channel of cross-fertilization of ideas. The meetings were generally informal and consisted of discussions of scholarly papers.

Henry P. Van Dusen sensed an emerging consensus among the group, and in 1945 he edited a collection of essays by its members entitled *The Christian Answer*.[15] Tillich contributed the lead piece, "The World Situation." This essay represents Tillich's most complete social analysis of the late war years. The outcome of the war was clear by the time he wrote in 1944, but the atomic bomb and the overt split between Russia and the US were not yet in evidence.

Though Van Dusen's introduction to the volume emphasizes the original process by which the essays were written, criticized, and rewritten, the content of Tillich's essay is not really new. Much of the argument is from *The Religious Situation*, which had been published in Germany in 1926, and other material is from a manuscript that remained in fragment form. Tillich had begun work on a volume on "Religion and World Politics," which was to be published in German by a Dutch publishing firm. The outbreak of the war ended that project, but much of the conceptual argument appears in "The World Situation" and the original fragment is available in

---

[15] *The Christian Answer*, ed. Henry P. Van Dusen (New York: Charles Scribner's Sons, 1945).

German and in Matthew Lon Weaver's translation.[16] Some of Tillich's characteristic dialectic disappeared under Van Dusen's editing, and the claims for the ecumenical church sometimes seem to owe more to Van Dusen than to Tillich.[17] However, the essay, which has been reprinted for popular distribution,[18] remains one of Tillich's most important statements on social philosophy from his American writings.

The work is an attempt by a Westerner to discover the meaning of a revolution that is absorbing the whole world. The determining fact of the emerging, interconnected world is seen as the bourgeois triumph over feudalism and subsequent control over the fate of the world and, most importantly, the ensuing revolt against bourgeois life. World War II is presented as the absorption of the world in the struggle of forces arising out of the failure of bourgeois society to provide security and meaning.

In monopoly capitalism armed with technology, humanity had created a Leviathan that was nearly irresistible. The chaos of bourgeois economic life and the wars of the twentieth century, says Tillich, refute the myth of laissez-faire harmony, and society is now in revolt against liberal capitalism. In Italy and Germany it is a Fascist revolt; in the US and England it takes the form of New Deal planning and mild socialist measures; and in Russia, communism expresses the revolt. Humanity could not return to the capitalism of recurrent depressions, Tillich argues, so planning is inevitable. Tillich, however, hopes for an order that will avoid "totalitarian absolutism" and "liberal individualism." The danger he sees ahead is the

[16] Paul Tillich, *Gesammelte Werke* (Stuttgart: Evangelisches Verlagswerk, 1959-75), 9:139-92. See Matthew Lon Weaver, *Religious Internationalism: War and Peace in the Thought of Paul Tillich* (Macon: Mercer University Press, 2010).

[17] Paul Tillich, *The World Situation*, Social Ethics Series, no. 2 (Philadelphia: Fortress Press, 1965).

[18] Tillich, *World Situation*, 24.

modern Leviathan, totalitarianism.

In "The World Situation," Tillich shows how personality and community evolve together. His analysis ranges over art, family structure, and education, revealing that the political-economic substance of a culture dominates these cultural expressions. Politics and economics are interdependent, he says, and cannot be separated. Much of postwar Christian social ethics would have had more depth if this interdependence of economics and politics had been kept in view.

Throughout the essay, Tillich's concern for structures that would protect the masses from economic insecurity emerges. His own early experience among the workers in Berlin inclines his writing in favor of security for the masses, and he calls for breaking the power of "large vested interests.[19] Christianity, he argues, must be committed in its struggle against dehumanization to an alliance with the masses for economic reorganization of the system.

Tillich was not an absolutist in defense of democracy as a constitutional form of government. He thought that liberal democracy demanded prerequisites that were not present in most of the world. The basic principle of his political ethics was the rendering of justice to the "dignity of every human being."[20] A distinction must be made, he argued, between the constitutional system of democracy and democracy as the protection of human dignity. Christianity was allied to the latter cause, but not necessarily to any political form. His colleague Reinhold Niebuhr wrote *The Children of Light and the Children of Darkness* at about this same time.[21] As an American with a different experience of democracy, Niebuhr offered a more thoroughgoing defense of democracy. The two were very close in politics, but Niebuhr was more of a radical democrat than Tillich and,

[19] Tillich, 26.

[20] Tillich, 27.

[21] Reinhold Niebuhr, *The Children of Light and the Children of Darkness* (New York: Charles Scribner's Sons, 1944).

after the war, more prone than Tillich to a Cold War defense of democracy. Christianity for Tillich could not sanction forms of democracy that hid the "destruction of community and personality."

The old balance of power politics of nineteenth century Europe was inadequate for the twentieth century. Tillich saw hope resting in a federation of nations not overly dominated by the victorious allies, but the world lacked the unifying spirit to make such a federation a reality. Christianity had to commit itself to the building of a common spirit within the world. Such a task required an inclusive, ecumenical Christianity. Existential and universal truth would need to be unified within an inclusive church if the church were to rise to the occasion demanded by the world situation.

He summarized the situation: a world revolution was under way against a decaying bourgeois order. Christianity had to protect the masses from meaninglessness and insecurity by promoting a new order. Such an agenda required an ecumenical, progressive Christianity, which remained realistic in the midst of tragedy and eschewed utopian solutions. Tillich's vision during the closing years of the war was essentially the same as during the years of the Weimar Republic. The victory of an autonomous humanity was affirmed in all its radicalness. Solutions of returning to totalitarian heteronomy were to be avoided even when autonomy was threatening, but humanity had to move on to a theonomous culture in which a modern solution for people in community could be found.

Across the street from the Union Seminary Tower in which Tillich wrote his philosophy, another group was working on the atomic bomb. The headquarters of the Manhattan Project, located on the campus of Columbia University, was visible from Union. The detonation of the world's first two atomic bombs on Japan would close the war but plunge humanity into a new, revolutionary, world situation.

The most passionately expressed war aim of Paul Tillich is the destruction of Nazism. This is paralleled by the liberation of Europe which is to be also the liberation of Germany. As in classical just-war theory there was the just cause and also the punishment of evil. In the speeches *Against the Third Reich* these goals are expressed with a fervor and connection with the ultimate, appearing to give the struggle the appearance of a crusade. Other war aims in *Against the Third Reich* are the establishment of a world federation, federation in Europe including Germany, social-economic security for the masses, and freedom in its human rights forms and also in its constitutional forms.

He saw the outcome of the war as a victory for Christianity over both Nazism and secularism and as a victory for Anglo-American democracy and Russian communism. He dreaded the colonization of Germany by the victors and hoped for its avoidance. He did not share these fears with his German listeners who already feared the consequences of losing the war.

Elsewhere I have written on Tillich as a theologian of peace. In this war he is a participant against the evil dominating his homeland. He is not a fully developed just-war theorist, though he believes World War II to be both necessary and justifiable on the part of the allies. His attempts to persuade Franklin D. Roosevelt not to pursue unconditional surrender and to listen to the needs of the German resistance for less demanding terms were rebuffed. His protests against the attacks on civilians were not accepted. In the end he acquiesced and interpreted the destruction of their cities as punishment for Nazi evil and told his listeners that they could not expect to negotiate with the democracies before surrendering their arms. His is the Christian realism that seeks peace as far as it is possible, and then participates in war with few illusions about limiting the violence. Yet he seeks to limit it. In trying to define the war aims he hopes to help shape the war settlements toward longer periods of no war.

Tillich's articulation of war aims for World War II in various contexts still provides an agenda for this century. The world still seeks ways to provide human security for the masses. The reality of hundreds of thousands of people suffering from malnutrition and the denial of resources to become fully human thwarts claims for justice or peace. Still we seek to mold a Europe that will contain a peaceful Germany. Can we continue to contain Germany in a larger NATO and a European Union? The goal of a world organization that can restrain nations from war still eludes us. The fate of the Jewish people still hangs in the balance though now it is dangers in the Middle East rather than in Europe that threaten them. Our ecumenical religious unity that could undergird world ethics for peace and promote human solidarity remains a dream threatened by ethnic idolatries. Many of his ideals couched in realism remain utopian. But the very process of defining war aims remains a needed exercise. Failure to be clear about war aims leads to disaster in Vietnam, Somalia, Central America, uncertainty and vagueness against Iraq, and vacillation or uncertainty in the former Yugoslavia. Peacemakers, too, whether at the United Nations or in the United States, need reinforcement in the pursuit of rigor in defining how and when they will defend peace or fight for peacemaking and justice.

Chapter 6

CRITIQUE OF JOHN F. DULLES' COMMISSION ON A JUST AND DURABLE PEACE[1]

By 1943, The Federal Council of Churches Commission on a Just and Durable Peace, under the strong leadership of John Foster Dulles, had completed its preliminary work. The commission invited Tillich to deliver three lectures to help shape the Commission's theological work. Though Dulles' strong hand guided the work of the Commission, he realized his inability to do the theological work that the Commission needed. The work of the Commission never took the shape consistent with either John C. Bennett or Reinhold Niebuhr, but their influence is seen in the invitation to Paul Tillich. Signs of Tillich's lectures are also not apparent in the work of the Commission. His three lectures remained obscure until I found them in the Tillich Archives of the Andover-Harvard Library at

[1] This chapter was originally published as Ronald H. Stone, "Paul Tillich's Critique of John F. Dulles' Commission on a Just and Durable Peace," in *Brokenness and Reconciliation, International Yearbook for Tillich Research*, vol. 14, eds. Christian Danz, Marc Dumas, Werner Schüßler, and Bryan Wagoner (Berlin, De Gruyter, 2020), 203-14.

Harvard Divinity School. They were handwritten, and Dr. Mutie Tillich Farris resisted publishing them until I persuaded her that they were really against the grain of Dulles' work, even though given to his Commission.

The war had turned against the Axis powers in 1942, and its end could be glimpsed in 1943. It was time to prepare the peace. The Federal Council of Churches had entrusted their work to Dulles' commission fortified by leading Christian thinkers. Though Tillich and Dulles differed significantly, there were points of contact between them. They were both sons of prominent ministers, one Lutheran and one Calvinist. They were both in World War I, though Dulles role was confined to a desk in military intelligence while Tillich served as a German chaplain in the trenches. Tillich feasted on the thought of Friedrich Schelling while Dulles picked up aspects of his thought in his study in Paris with Henri Bergson. Dulles' award winning Princeton thesis on pragmatism was foreign material for Tillich at this time as he mined his German idealist roots. Dulles was on the Board of Directors of Union Theological Seminary, which nurtured the exiled Tillich. Dulles' father had taught at Auburn Seminary, which merged with Union. The father of Allen Dulles and John Foster Dulles urged the boys to enter the Presbyterian ministry, but they followed the coaching of their Grandfather toward law and the Foreign Service. Dulles' defense of the liberal Henry Pitney van Dusen from Presbyterian heresy charges separated him from the more conservative Princeton theologians and placed him, broadly speaking, in the Union camp. They had both been leaders in the 1937 Oxford Conference on church and society in the disordered civilization. As late as 1952, Dulles, before assuming the responsibilities as Secretary of State, addressed the conference for ministry at Union Theological Seminary, and he and President van Dusen remained friends for their lives. Their family roots were middle class though they were familiar with association with top leadership. Dulles was happy with his capitalism, and fundamental to Tillich in 1943 was his socialist critique of capitalism.

In 1943, Allen Dulles was beginning his association with the German opposition to Hitler which he named "The Breakers." Allen reported on the underground from his position in Bern, Switzerland. Tillich received messages from the underground among his German friends exiled in New York City, and he tried to apprise Roosevelt of the seriousness of the underground and his opposition to "Unconditional Surrender" demands. Tillich was friends with Eleanor Roosevelt, the more progressive of the Roosevelts, while Dulles' in 1943 was associating with churchmen and preparing to lobby President Roosevelt on behalf of the Commission's recommendations for the United Nations. Tillich's critique is best appreciated from the vantage point of understanding his mind in 1943 and the presuppositions of Dulles and the work of the Commission.

Paul Tillich's self-consciousness in 1943 was that of a German in exile developing an organization for refugees from Europe. He thought of himself as a socialist and a protestant. In addition to his Union Seminary and Columbia University courses, which he was teaching in his new English, he was editing a journal and weekly producing anti-Hitler speeches for the Voice of America. European refugees frequented his apartment on 122nd Street, and in the evenings he had an office across Broadway to manage Self-Care for Central European Refugees.

His policy statement for the journal in 1942 set the stage for his criticism of the pride of John Foster Dulles' Commission on a Just and Durable Peace. God's majesty was not to be captured by church, government, or political party. Prophetic protest is to be raised against all claims to absolutism. The divine is related to all human activity, and the sacred and secular are not separate realms. The churches should not encroach upon the spheres of the cultural life to dominate them. However, all of culture is undergirded by spiritual life, and cultural immanence is not independent of religious transcendence. Christian ethics is relevant to all politics as demand and criticism, but there is no final Christian system of politics. Dulles' Commission needed theological help, but it was not ready for either Tillich's sophistication or his paradoxical approach to political-ethical discourse.

Tillich's theological existentialism is a little muted in his formal lectures to the Dulles' Commission, but during the same year it is apparent in his war speeches delivered weekly in German over the Voice of America. These speeches called for Germans to turn against the Nazis and to join the effort to liberate Europe. They deal with the destruction coming to Germany and the Nazis compact with death for Germany. They are talks of the theology of guilt, destruction, and liberation. His focus on the centrality of anti-Semitism to Nazi ideology and the horrendous crimes against the Jews was central to his thought. The passion of the German warrior who holds in his mind the synthesis of German culture, European humanism, and Christian heritage calls for Germany to die and then seek resurrection in its struggle against Nazism. Themes of Dr. Faustus, German history, the meaning of Good Friday, the promise of Easter, and German mourning over losses at Stalingrad are woven together in a theology of European liberation and the remaking of Europe. The passionate theology of the war speeches needs to be read together with Tillich's lectures to the ecclesiastical and future political establishments of the United States to understand the paradoxical quality of his political ethics. He understood the ambiguity of both the Germans and the Americans in the war.

THE COMMISSION ON A JUST AND DURABLE PEACE

Dulles had grasped the importance of religion in international affairs in 1937 at the Oxford Conference on Civilization and its disorder. His words reflected the change:

> During that period it did not seem to me that what I had learned here in church had much to do with the practical problems of war

> and peace. That was indeed my state of mind for thirty years, from 1907 when I attended with my grandfather the second Hague Peace Conference until 1937. In that year I presided at an internarial peace conference held at Paris under the auspices of the League of Nations, and then went on to attend the Oxford Conference on Church and State. We discussed there the same critical problems that diplomats were discussing futilely at the League of Nations. But at Oxford we approached these problems with the guidance of a common standard—the moral law as revealed by Jesus Christ; and we dealt with each other as brothers, irrespective of national or racial differences....Then I began to understand the profound significance of the spiritual values that my father and mother taught and by which they lived here at Watertown. From then on I began to work closely with religious groups—Protestant, Catholic, and Jewish—for I had come to believe that of all groups, they could make the greatest contribution to world order.[2]

Oxford represented a turning point for John Foster Dulles and, though unknown at the time, for the church's witness in international relations. Even at Oxford, where Dulles found his own concern for world order matched by the churchmen and he chose to become one of them, he did not play a passive role. He delivered a paper stressing the inevitability of change and the necessity of channeling dynamic forces into peaceful pursuits. Edward Duff recognized Dulles' influence there by writing: "Mr. Dulles' mind and hand can be seen also in the Oxford emphasis on the need of provisions for peaceful change in the international order."3 Paul Tillich, who was also producing a paper for the conference, would have had no difficulty with this emphasis on change, but the tendency toward appeasement seen in Dulles' essay was anathema to Tillich.

Dulles' brilliance, energy and drive soon led him to propose a commission on international affairs for the Federal Council of

---

[2] "Faith of our Fathers," in *The Spiritual Legacy of John Foster Dulles,* ed. Henry P. Van Dusen (Philadelphia: The Westminster Press, 1960), 6-7.

[3] Edward Duff, *The Social Thought of the World Council of Churches* (London: Longmans, Green and Co., 1986), 262.

Churches. In addressing the council he said:

> There is before you an opportunity which is unique. There is also a responsibility which is heavy. For the churches of Christ, in America represent the most powerful body of Christian influence in the world.[4]

The Council adopted, with some amendment, Dulles' proposal, and he was made chairman of the Commission for a Just and Durable Peace. During the Commission's life it was dominated by Dulles. There were other strong men present and they, particularly John Bennett and Reinhold Niebuhr, were responsible for asking Tillich to address the commission's work. John Bennett told me how humbled he was at Union by lecturing at 10:00 a.m. between Niebuhr's earlier lecture and Tillich's lecture following Bennett's class, but here they were together for Tillich's presentations in 1943.

For purposes of analysis Jessie Burroway divided the Commission's work into four periods.5 For two years it restricted its work to defining moral principles and instituting educational movements to win support for its principles. During the spring of 1943 the Commission translated its moral principles into broad political propositions. By the summer of 1943 the Commission chose to put its prestige behind various concrete proposals for international organizations. The ratification of the UN Charter was followed by the Commission's efforts to support the organization and to influence its direction. Tillich's lectures were designed to move from Christian principles to broad political propositions between the first and second stages. Later, when feeling political pressure from the churches, Dulles would try to confine the church to the first stage of the

---

[4] John Foster Dulles, "The American churches in Time of War," *Federal Council Bulletin* 24 (January 1941), 6.

[5] Jessie J. Burroway, "*Christian Witness Concerning World Order: The Federal Council of Churches and Postwar Planning: 1941-1947*" (doctoral dissertation, University of Michigan, 1953), 14-17.

Commission's work.[6] Part of the problem was, of course, that Dulles failed to note in his earlier confession after Oxford that part of the difference between statesmen and churchmen is that the statesmen are restricted to their country's national interest as defined by their president or ruler whereas the churchman has a different master.

The early guiding principles were drafted by Dulles and approved by the Delaware Study Conference of the Federal Council. The thirteen principles were grounded in recognition of moral law founded by God and revealed in the "simple" teachings of Jesus Christ. Dulles read the New Testament with a lawyer's mind, and he regarded the synoptic gospel teachings of Jesus about the moral law as obligatory for American Christians who were called to fulfill their responsibilities.[7] The principles called for law to regulate economics, treaties, armaments, colonies, and international relations. This law was regarded as analogous to physical law even if it was not defined rigorously. It was an American version of natural law theory designed to promote internationalism by American citizens of Christian faith.[8] These principles were formulated before Tillich spoke to the Commission, and after his lectures the principles were reduced to the "Six Pillars of Peace." These Six Pillars of Peace became the foundation for the Federal Council of Churches' campaign

[6] "I recall particularly the Study Conference held at Delaware, Ohio, in 1942....As we said at that tune, the churches do not have a primary responsibility to devise the details of world order. They do have a responsibility to provide the enduring moral principles by which governmental action as well as private action should consistently be inspired and tested." John Foster Dulles, *Principles and Policies in a Changing World* (Washington D.C.: Department of State, 1958), 1.

[7] John Foster Dulles, "Statement of Guiding Principles," in *A Righteous Faith for a Just and Durable Peace* (New York: Commission to Study the Basis for a Just and Durable Peace, 1942), 104.

[8] Walter Horton indicated in preparing the studies for the Amsterdam Assembly that the principles were based on a natural law approach. See Duff, *Social Thought*, 109.

to win the United Nation's establishment and to guide its educational programs. The Six Pillars could all be found in Dulles' earlier book, *War, Peace and Change.*[9] While Tillich would not have denied any of the Six Pillars, they represented Dulles' legal background and his satisfaction and optimism about international organization which Tillich's Christian realism denied. The Pillars expected continued collaboration among the allies in: the regulation of international economics, the revision of treaties to changing conditions, the freeing of the colonies, the controlling internationally of national armaments, and universal religious liberty.[10] Called in to lecture to assist the Commission in its theological work, he challenged the foundations of Dulles' Commission. Tillich was much more informed than Dulles about Marxist theory. He was influenced by it. He drew on the concept of World War II as part of world revolution. Dulles, as a successful capitalist and Presbyterian, was set against Marxism as his teacher Woodrow Wilson and his Secretary of State grandfather had been. However his reading of J.V. Stalin's *The Problems of Leninism*[11] was still in the future. With the Korean War and the reading of Stalin, Dulles' anti-communism became polemical. In 1943 he still dreamed of allied cooperation and built his program of the development of a strong United Nations upon it. Tillich as a Social Democrat could think of working with communists in a new Germany, but I do not think, and his writing does not show, that he expected collaboration. Dulles learned later that any collaboration by Stalin and his successors was only tactical as they expected to overthrow imperialist capitalism, of which John

[9] John Foster Dulles, *A Righteous Faith*, 10.

[10] John Foster Dulles, "Statement of Political Principles," in *Statements on World Order (*New York: Commission to Study the Basis of a Just and Durable Peace, 1943), 13.

[11] J.V. Stalin, *Problems of Leninism* (Peking: Foreign Language Press, 1976) or J.V. Stalin, " The Foundations of Leninism" in *Works* VI (Moscow Foreign Language House Publishing House, 1924) 71-196.

Foster Dulles was a prime example.

TILLICH'S LECTURES

Tillich's 1943 lectures to the Commission on a Just and Durable Peace sought to define the Commission's work as theological thought and social analysis. They were eclipsed by the work of the Commission and the chair's overly simple reading of principles derived from Jesus' teaching. The lectures were first published in 1980.[12]

Tillich feared an overly direct movement from theology to politics as it might support either pacifism or militarism. The relationship between theology and politics recognized the broken gap between the two in their relationship to each other.

Principles of theology are not doctrines but requirements of thought inherent to doctrine that guide the analysis and prevent mistakes. The formal principles are expressed in the life of the church as: (1) "absolute transcendence of the divine," (2) the paradoxical immanence of the divine, and (3) the "universal reference of the divine."[13]

Transcendence is found in the first commandment, and it denies false idols and ideologies. It prohibits claims to divinity or the finding of it in political programs or in some future utopia. Immanence affirms historical reality while finding it unfulfilled while continuing transcendence within it. All is from God, but it is not God. The universal reference to God means all is related to God with no escape to a dualism of good spiritual and evil material. It challenges both religious idolatry and secular pride and protests against hierarchies and individual isolation.

---

[12] Paul Tillich, *Theology of Peace*, ed. Ronald H. Stone (Louisville: Westminster/John Knox Press, 1980), 73-87. The original, handwritten, lectures can be found in the Paul Tillich Papers at the Andover-Harvard Theological Library.

[13] Tillich, 74-75.

The material principles of Christian life are love, power, and justice. Sometimes at this point he substitutes "life" for power, but the fuller argument returns to the three which later bear so much weight in *Love, Power, and Justice*, many speeches and essays, and finally in *Systematic Theology*.

Love contains the formal principles of transcendence, immanence, and universalism and is the ground of reality. Love as demands expresses not something foreign, but who we are essentially. Life or power is dynamic striving for self-realization. The only absolute power is God. There is no status quo, everything living moves and strives. There is no politics except power politics. Life or power requires justice.

Justice, then, is that which unites the dynamic expressions of being in a manner that leads to the fulfillment of being. It is not an imposed law, but the uniting of reality to the forces at work. So justice is the uniting form of politics. In 1943, of course, everything is disrupted by the defeated powers of Nazism which led to the destruction of Germany. The lack of justice in Germany created chaos. In Tillich's mind the world was in revolt against its old arrangements of bourgeois order. The de-colonial forces rocking India were an example. Dulles, Stalin, and Tillich all recognized the world in revolt. Dulles wanted the UN to evolve trusteeships and decolonization. Tillich was less dogmatic about his expectations. Stalin wanted to fish in the world confusion and seize opportunities to encourage movement toward the Russian-led worldwide dictatorship of the proletariat. Dulles advocated free capitalism and Stalin, Communism. Tillich hoped for a guided-state socialism meeting the needs of the masses and individuals. So for Tillich the concepts of "Just and Durable" were inadequate.

For Tillich the social problem was more fundamental than the nations clashing in war. Social justice would always be fragmentary and incomplete. But an effort needed to be made to work toward a "liberalized state capitalism." The dehumanization of monopoly capitalism produced an alienated humanity of dehumanization, to use the thought of the early Karl Marx. Peace, if it fit the meaning of the present crisis, was not best thought of in terms of "Just and Durable" which sounded like the pursuit of the status quo in a revolutionary world. His analysis pursued human dignity in the midst of collective production, so even in America at war his thought was not far from his German religious socialist roots in 1943. Tillich used the image of Thomas Hobbes' Leviathan to symbolize the politics of monopoly capitalism which utilized human reason against nature to force humans to adjust to its mores and meaninglessness. He rejected the conservative politics of England which in educational reform was trying to use religion to enforce conservative social policies in the United Kingdom. Rather he found hope in radical British politics, in the anti-Nazi underground in Europe, in the New Deal, in progressive churches, and, strangely, in Russia. He hoped for their alliance to prevent Leviathan-like repression in liberated Europe after the war.

He feared that possible gains of the war might be forfeited, as they were after World War I. He could not see beyond hopes for liberalized, state capitalism and the overcoming of monopoly capitalism. Much of the US was organized for its wartime economy in 1943. He did not expect large gains for his generation, but he hoped in the overcoming of monopoly capitalism there might be more human life for his children's generation. For his own homeland his words were more pessimistic as he saw mostly death and destruction for Germany in 1943.[14]

The last lecture featured Tillich's pessimism because the disordered society provided no basis for international peace. The incompleteness of the essay suggests the criticism by the Commission of his earlier socialist analysis. The world was disrupted, and destruction would precede any ordering. The possibilities of ordering were

[14] Tillich, *Against the Third Reich,* 107-222.

foreboding. It could be regional arrangements. Would the American-Anglo powers dominate everything in a liberal manner? What about Germany? Could it be rejuvenated or only occupied? The social disruptions from Europe to Asia left little expectation that a spirit of humanity could inspire people to find vocations for the common good.

The idea of world organization beyond the nation was inspired by the prophets who learned of a God beyond the fate of a nation. But the modern concept of world was of nations at war. The old imperialisms and the old balances of power seemed overcome in the destructive forces of international war. He read the current trends opposing the surrendering of national sovereignty in economics or politics. So hopes for international government could not be realized.

He found the ecumenical movement to be a sign of emerging world consciousness. But the churches lacked the power and the unity to achieve much. After all, the various churches reflected the social disease of the present and the national limitations. Secularism provided no alternative, as it lacked vision, but provided only various patterns of meaninglessness.

The world society of love was more transcendent than immanent as divine wrath was upon the warring nations. The tragedy must be endured before grace would be revealed in strength.

His conclusion argued that in light of Christian principles and prophetic tradition, the "moral arrogance" of the principles of a just and durable peace had been destroyed by his analysis. Tragedy and the possibility of grace were more appropriate concepts.[15] Arrogance was a frequent criticism of John Foster Dulles in both his character and his policies.

Dulles' Commission continued its work. The chair and his role as a bipartisan Republican chosen for sensitive international roles by

---

[15] Tillich, *Theology of Peace,* 87.

Democrats increased his power. He possessed both a role in a political party and in the church. Tillich's religious socialism had neither a party nor a church. The Cold War, which in 1943 could only be feared in dim appropriations of the danger, disrupted the work of both. It broke Tillich's Council for a Democratic Germany and disappointed Dulles' hopes for a strong United Nations. Dulles would use his Cold War anti-communist rhetoric to ride Democratic and Republican Presidents' coattails to gain immense political power. Dulles died before Eisenhower finished his second term. Tillich's political energy was renewed by the election of John F. Kennedy. His assassination rocked Tillich. He rallied to denounce the candidacy of Barry Goldwater for his saber rattling, and his last important political action was a critique of *Pacem in Terris* calling for more realism on the part of the Pope.

Tillich's assignment of blame to powers in the English and American worlds that were slow in disengaging from Hitler's economy did not please Dulles, who reluctantly disengaged his law firm from German profits at the insistence of other partners. Tillich's calls for Germans to resist Nazism in his Voice of America broadcasts were not supported by Roosevelt as a viable strategy. His distinctions between Nazis and Germans were not developed in American policy. His love of Germany, matched by his hatred of Nazism, was neither understood nor appreciated by the American government, which kept him under investigation and prevented him from returning to Germany until 1948. Even then his religious socialism was too radical for some ecumenical churchmen who kept him out of the ecumenical gathering in Amsterdam in 1948. What a meeting it could have been if both Tillich and Barth had given voice to their political theologies there in the meeting that expressed the Cold War between Dulles and the Czech theologian Hromadka.

My comment that religious socialism of Tillich's commitment had neither church nor party should not be taken to mean that Tillich lost all power. He extended his work helping refugees from

Hitler into Self Help for Emigres from Central Europe, which became the most significant refugee assistance nonprofit organization existing into the present. Tillich chaired the organization from its inception in 1936 until he left Union 15 years later. He counseled individuals, wrote letters, gave speeches, and brought a warm spirit of service to the individuals he assisted through the organization. The Pauck biography has a particularly warm description of his aid to Walter Mosse, for whom he found a position teaching German to PhD candidates in the doctoral programs of Union Theological Seminary and Columbia University. [16] I benefited from Mosse's teaching in 1964 when I was pursuing the PhD in Columbia. Tillich's own writing about this work is best found in Lefevre's collection of Tillich's essays.[17] The day to day work of providing "Good Samaritan" aid is vital social ministry. The year after criticizing the Dulles Commission, he founded The Council for a Democratic Germany. He wrote the founding declaration after Thomas Mann had turned down the chairmanship on the advice of the US government. It presupposed cooperation between Russia and the US. It advocated: the unity of a reconstructed Germany, the rebuilding of German economic power in the inclusion of a Federated Europe, the expurgation of Nazism, the reform of German education by Germans, and the empowerment of democracy. As the Cold War divided the refugees, the Council's life came to an end in 1945. Tillich later attributed his reduction of political activity to his disappointment over the Council's failure. The Paucks suggested he realized his religious socialism was too romantic for the times.[18] I think he wanted to preserve the place of utopia in his thought but to control it. They don't mention his continued support of socialism in Germany after the war, but Christopher Niebuhr wrote me that Tillich continued to send contributions to the SPD after the war. The

[16] Pauck and Pauck, *Paul Tillich*, 157-9.
[17] Paul Tillich, *The Meaning of Health*.
[18] Pauck and Pauck, *Paul Tillich*, 206.

return of democratic socialism to the debates about America's future since the 2016 elections provides a different context than that at the time of the Paucks' publication in 1976. Even his Germany is now reunited, although with different borders than Tillich knew in 1945 or 1933 when he migrated.

Tillich's reflections on the Dulles' Commission reflect his other writings at the time in: his "War Aims" for his journal, *The Protestant*; his speeches for the voice of America into occupied Europe; and Henry Pitney Van Dusen's *The World Situation.*[19] He feared a punitive occupation of Germany. He hoped for a liberal management of planned economies to overcome "monopoly capitalism". He urged an ecumenical, worldwide movement to encourage a religious vision of inspired people creating a wholesome economy in either regional or world federations. Economic security was a minimal aim of the war against the Leviathan of totalitarian government and capitalism, and a planned economics had to tend to the humanity of the person and a variety of human aspirations.

[19] See Ronald Stone, *Politics and Faith* (Macon: Mercer University Press, 2012), 150-9.

Chapter 7

POWER IN THE CONTEXT OF THE AMERICAN EMPIRE[1]

Tillich, as an officer in the German emperor's army, learned that Germany possessed power sufficient to defeat Russia but was unable to prevail against England, France, and the United States. Later, as a refugee, he saw Germany's power as adequate to absorb Austria and Czechoslovakia but inadequate to contain Poland when opposed by Russia, England, France, and, finally, the United States. As a Central European, he was free of utopian illusions that one empire could dominate the world. Still, as first a German and then a German-American he lived in two of the most powerful empires of history.

His political history and his theology of the power of the divine both drove him to reflect continually on power for his theology and his politics. This chapter will not delve into the tortured relationship

---

[1] This chapter was published in *International Yearbook for Tillich Research*, vol. 9, eds. Christian Danz, Marc Dumas, Werner Schüßler, Mary Ann Stenger, and Erdmann Sturm (Berlin: De Gruyter, 2014): 47-62.

of his theology and politics as a chaplain to the emperor's warriors. Nor will it attempt to analyze the terms for *power* in his German theology.

Kyle Pasewark has provided an adequate analysis of the relationship of *Kraft*, *Urkraft*, *Machtigkeit*, and *Macht* to the one American word power.[2] The American translators of Tillich's early ontological and socialist writings will need to tread carefully as they prepare their translations for the projected *The Complete Works of Paul Tillich*. In the breadth of his writings within the American Empire the nuances of the term *power* from the power of being to power politics require interpretation from the context.

Pasewark's definition of power as communicative efficacy has much to commend it. He moved to the definition by embracing Foucault's abandonment of political theory and by affirming Luther's communion doctrine of the body. Paul Tillich preferred symbols of Christ to "real presence" and knew of other approaches to political theory. Pasewark's following of Foucault's attempt to reduce political theory to regarding power as domination was unfortunate. Liberal theories from John Locke to James Madison, and *The Federalist Papers*, regarded sovereignty more on the basis of participation than domination.

Pasewark's rejection of power as residing in a government or a person is overly simple. Tillich's definition of power as both potential and applied is superior, though admitting some ambiguity to Pasewark's insistence that power is only present at the borders of encounters. Pasewark affirms Tillich's ontology of power and his realization that power is ubiquitous. He wants only to free Tillich from the idea of power as centered in either a person or a government. I think Tillich's ontology of the power of being and political power is dynamic enough and relational enough to meet Pasewark's

[2] Kyle A. Pasewark, *A Theology of Power: Being Beyond Domination* (Minneapolis: Fortress Press, 1993), 272-86.

objections to it. For those not content with either Foucault or Luther's perspective on power, Tillich's ontology and politics hold up well within the context of the American Empire.

To use an analogy from boxing: every boxer eyeing his opponent in the opposite corner knows there is power in both corners. That power will be expressed in the relationship of combat, skill, and morale. Communicative efficacy is totally inadequate to describe the reality of power in the ring or in many other human relationships. Justice governs the contest through the agreed upon rules. Love is absent as there is no urge to unite the two boxers but rather the use of coercion to decide the outcome through rules.

Tillich humorously speculated that American listeners to his lectures on power might think he was speaking about electricity. Knowing now how computers and our brains are driven by electrical charges, his musings seem less whimsical. The power grids of the Tennessee Valley Authority and our capacity to produce power by plugging into a socket are probably not best described as communicative efficacy.

Despite his attempts to recognize that much of Tillich's discussion of realized power presupposed human estrangement, Pasewark's work remains more at the essential level than Tillich's writing. Pasewark wants to avoid utopianism and realpolitik. So did Tillich. Tillich's faithful realism avoids both of Pasewark's poles while retaining an ethic of hopeful realism.

There remains the question of whether justice is outside of power. Pasewark believes it has to be an expression of power. That is true, for the power of being expresses justice. But in human affairs applied justice is an estranged power representing the interests and history of the crooked timber of humanity. Tillich was wiser, maintaining a relationship between power and justice without collapsing one into the other.

THE PROBLEM OF POWER

Reinhold Niebuhr fussed that the translations in Tillich's *The Interpretation of History* should never have been accepted by the publisher.[3] This is certainly true of the chapter on power. Niebuhr retranslated the introduction, "On the Boundary," elegantly, thereby making the book publishable. But he could only invest so many hours in the project, and the other chapters are what they are, though they will have to be retranslated for *The Complete Works*.

Paul Tillich's essay on power was published in 1931 in a socialist journal. The life struggle for power illustrated in the essay is between Socialism and National Socialism. The struggle dominates the introduction and the powerful conclusion of the essay. In between, Tillich presents his ontology of power.[4]

Fearing that revolutionary socialism was overly dependent on bourgeois concepts of power, he set out to clarify the concept. Admitting he could not do more than introduce the problem, he appealed to political thinkers to complete the important task. At the time, as Professor of Philosophy and Sociology in Frankfurt, he was immersed in political theorists who might have undertaken the task. Power as a concept has its roots in the encounters of existence. Comets thrown from the beginning of the solar system that illumine our night skies and burn up in the sun's gravity express power. Or as American policy vis-à-vis Israel draws our drones to kill people in Pakistan, expressing force without the perception of justice, the drone policy is only force without power as more enemies are produced than killed. Tillich saw everything in existence meeting in

---

[3] Ursula Niebuhr, ed., *Remembering Reinhold Niebuhr* (San Francisco: HarperSanFrancisco, 1991), 89.

[4] Paul Tillich, "The Problem of Power" in *The Interpretation of History* (New York: Charles Scribner's Sons, 1936), 179-202.

encounters and advancing or retreating to maintain unity. Through Marx he learned of the dialectical principle of social tension. "All being is indeed a balance of tensions or might, then social being is a balance of tensions of power."[5] Human consciousness and will shape the struggle of life, forming structures of power in a balance. The leading group organizes the will of the whole group to express itself for the group's power. This power depends upon the combination and demand.

Tillich expects society to be uniform only in primitive societies or in future static societies. In this world neither the law nor the bureaucracy expresses all of the wills of the society, but rather those of the leading group. He may not at this point yet understand how law and bureaucracy are the result of compromise and tradition. He argued that the law expressed the interests of the group in power.

Power is related to forces in society. Spiritual or ideological expressions that do not represent social forces have no power. If the social factors are present, ideas may organize those forces. Ideas without groups may be interesting, but they are without power.

In Tillich's view, power is maintained by acknowledgment of consent and force. The use of force or the threat of it is necessary to assure the union of the society. Revolutions happen when the real powers in a society replace the formal power.

Tillich, in 1931, regarded the nation-states as the most powerful actors maintaining their social existence. He must have included the reality of powerful empires within his claim for nation-states. He recognized evolving legal structures in the League of Nations, but they were still dependent upon the nation-states. Other international bodies like churches, businesses, intellectual groups, and the proletariat lacked unity or social power to overcome the nation-states.

Tillich saw Socialism as renouncing power and force and

[5] Tillich, 183.

National Socialism as exalting force. Neither position was correct. Socialism needed to learn from National Socialism to take power more seriously. It needed to realize that the renunciation of power was a false bourgeoisie idea that disguised the reality of its own power. In the social struggle Socialism needed to express the ideas that united it while at the same time grasping the instruments of power and winning the consent, even if reluctantly, from other groups.

Tillich knew that realism about power is never sufficient. He strove through his ontology to present a faithful realism. Pushing through the phenomena of political struggles he could perceive the ultimate in life's foundations, in crises and in norms. The norms are signals of transcendence. He included: justice in the prophetic sense, love, classless society, and world consciousness of the identity of all. He argued that these norms had to be taught continually in relevant ways to the powers.

The significant British historian, W.R. Ward, found Tillich's categories too abstract to be of political use. Reinhold Niebuhr, on the other hand, found his abstractions to be of the real stuff of life. Not surprisingly, Niebuhr has the better of the argument, and he is much closer to Tillich than Ward. Tillich's paragraphs on power are placed in a particular position in the wide-ranging debates among many socialist Christians of the Weimar period. John Clayton, while admiring Ward's work, finds it overly critical of Tillich's writing. Furthermore, he criticized Ward for relying too much upon Breipahl's contentious and misguided interpretation of Tillich's *Die Sozialtische Entscheidung of 1933.*[6] Ward had regarded Tillich as the foremost intellectual among the religious socialists but described his reduction of politics to a conceptual game. By the time of *The Socialist Decision* (1933), Tillich had been reduced to a man without

[6] W.R. Ward, *Theology, Sociology and Politics: The German Protestant Social Conscience 1890-1933* (Berne: Peter Lang Publishers, 1979).

political influence in either church or party. But that influence would be regained in the United States.

THE SOCIALIST DECISION

The presentation at the Hochschule fur Politik directed by his friend Arnold Wolfers produced the essay "die Macht" which was then incorporated in *Die Sozialtische Entsheidung*. The threat of National Socialism led Tillich, conferring with Adolph Lowe, to rush the book to conclusion. It was the book put on the first Black List of publications and the one he was urged to recant in exchange for a Professorship at the University of Berlin.[7]

Power in "The Socialist Decision" is analyzed from its roots in the myths of humanity to the contemporary crisis in Germany. The middle class parties in Germany are fragmented, and the Socialist Party is divided. The conservative parties are drifting toward political romanticism on the one hand and irrelevance on the other. The National Socialists understood force, and their mixture of romantic nationalism and myth threatens to draw in support from the bourgeois and the conservatives. The proletariat cannot exert their will unilaterally, and their alliances are weak. They reach neither the farmers nor the nationalists as their industrial urban base and universalistic ideology drive both away. Moreover, the socialist antipathy toward the church offends the traditionally religious.

Tillich had only recently joined the Socialist Party. He was alienated from his conservative church background by both lifestyle and politics. Still he urged the reform of both the church and the party. The "Socialist Principle" controls the argument. For him, the key to the Socialist Principle was realistic expectation. Expectation was distinguished from utopianism by its grounding in real, historical facts. It combined myths of creation of original humanity and prophetic criticism for a realistic hope. He hoped such an

[7] Ward, *Theology, Sociology, and Politics*, 215.

affirmation and program would draw National Socialists toward socialism. It could overcome the free thinking criticism of religion associated with socialism. Hope and realism together could unify the Socialists to overcome both the determinists and the activists in the concept and expectation of *kairos*.[8]

So here power was correlated with justice. Force and democracy were both means toward justice in a classless society. Justice would be partially realized if the will of the proletariat were allied to the wills of other groups sufficient to express a unified will through a national government. He saw himself, as he regarded Marx and Lenin, transcending biographical class to speak to the leading group of Germany.

The theory of social power Tillich explains is quite elitist. A leading social group gains power by unifying societies' will. Other groups will submit to the group gaining power by its superiority. The consent of the subjected is the basis of power. If force has to be relied upon, then power is contested and not fully realized yet. Consent does not have to be explicit, but it must realize enough human fulfilment so the leadership is conceded to the leading group. "So the problem of power proves to be the problem of a concrete justice."[9]

It is not for Socialism to criticize other historical periods' failures of justice in abstract natural law terms. Periods of history must be judged by their own standards of justice. The standard for the proletariat is the classless society which will govern by that standard. Proletarian leaders will need to be held accountable by democratic corrections of the classless society. Power will express the classless society as the general will of the nation drawing upon its expression of the human origins and its own goals. The stages of the "dictatorship of the proletariat" is for Tillich the victory of Socialism which

---

[8] John Stumme, introduction to *The Socialist Decision*, by Paul Tillich (San Francisco: Harper & Row Publishers, 1977), xxiv.

[9] Stumme, 141.

will eliminate the hidden power elites of the bourgeois society and produce new accountable leadership through democratic means to achieve the social goals. Even though Socialist goals and programs have to be worked out behind the scenes, they must be coordinated with the wills of other groups to govern.

In this essay, Tillich expresses the unity between the "young Marx" and the economist Marx. He combines a Marxist realism with Rousseau's theories of general will to propose a realistic picture of power groups held accountable to agreed upon standards. He sees his concept of expectation replacing utopian ideas of either the hard or the soft version of utopia. Power is the capacity to impose and correlate a group's will to the wills of other groups through force, democracy, and justice, as the situation requires.

WARTIME SPEECHES

Tillich's wartime speeches broadcast into Europe continue the use of power that he had developed in Frankfurt. Power is the capacity to persuade others to accept one's will. Sometimes in the wartime talks, power comes to mean force in the form of armed might. But force without "justice" cannot survive and Nazi devotion to force to destroy justice is doomed to defeat at the hands of the world allied against it.

Matthew Lon Weaver, an editor of the wartime speeches, entitled the speech of October 13, 1942 "Power Politics." Tillich had seen Hitler turn from conquest to a futile defense of that which he had conquered. The change revealed the limits of power as force without justice. Power is limited, and the resistance of the conquered peoples, combined with the allied forces, demonstrated those limits. All over Europe those rendered powerless were finding power and rising up to contest the power of their Nazi conquerors. Those rendered powerless found power in suffering for the justice Nazism betrayed.

The National Socialists came to power promising justice, but they really sought only power. So they were doomed to fail. Without the false promise of justice the Nazis could not have risen to power. The Nazis, with a promise to unify a powerful Germany, overthrew justice, and now fearing defeat they used the tools of power with ferociousness. The worship of power led them to see death, whereas the fruit of justice is life. The power of Nazism is undermined, but it will use the tools of power through the state to wreak havoc and destruction.

By April 6, 1943, Tillich focused on the limits upon tyrannical power. He spread the news to his German-speaking listeners of the increasing resistance to Nazi domination of the subjected peoples of Europe.

The Nazis succeeded in developing instruments of tyranny which seemed unlimited, but now the system was cracking at the joints. Authentic rule is dependent upon the serial agreement of the people governed. Nazism broke the will of the people who were its subjects. Nazism must break the will of those who oppose it, but they could not, and resistance became stronger. The oppression engendered more resistance, which encouraged more oppression, and the denial of the will of the people cycled down in its oppression, seeking its own destruction.

War, for a time, is a unifying national force, but the opposition of the unified world will overcome the warring Germany. Germans had given in to one of the most frightening tyrannies of all time, and the tyranny encouraged the world to organize against Germany. The Germans' own guilt in tolerating Hitler was bringing about their own destruction.

Later, the next month, Tillich argued the fate of Germany was to lose its power. He urged his listeners to accept their fate. He advised them to give up supporting Nazism and to join the resistance. The worship of power, he argued, was a fault of the German peoples' character. A less obedient, less servile people would have prevented the megalomaniac from taking the tools of state power. Something new can be made out of Germany after its defeat. Often, he pled for Germans to accept the death of their nation so that something new could be reborn.

In 1944, he wrote about community and power. Community, like other necessary and good entities, can be misused. Nazis misused the idea of national community to gain power. Of course, community, like all of life, requires power and is a source of power. But the Nazis used community for their own interests. The Nazi debasement of community meant that the only true German community remaining was in the opposition to Nazism. Real community required communal trust.

The Nazis in their mad rush for power destroyed the communities of marriage, family, friendship, neighborhoods, youth associations, and church. There was little time left for Nazi Germany, which had no common goal except the Nazi hold on power, which led to death. True German community was forming against Hitler. But Germany, Tillich said, in his Easter message for 1944, had to die so that it could be resurrected in spirit.

LOVE, POWER, AND JUSTICE[10]

The Tillich Harvard archive has a large collection of outlines and texts of speeches he gave on power and love or justice. These talks were combined to produce the book on love, power, and justice in 1953. He had thought about these concepts most of his career. In this small book he draws upon his dissertations, his reading of Nietzsche in World War I, and his understanding of Shakespeare and the power politics that drove him into exile. The clarification of the concepts is an exercise in linguistic analysis in the light of his ontological reflections on being. Tillich's explication of ontology in his second chapter moves into existentialism as he wrestles with

[10] Paul Tillich, *Love, Power, and Justice* (New York: Oxford University Press, 1954).

Kierkegaard on love, and in the third chapter he explores the ontology of Heidegger and Nietzsche.[11] The will to power is seen as the drive toward self-fulfillment. It is distinguished from "sociological power, namely the chance to carry through one's will against social resistance."[12]

Power is used to describe the ultimate. "Being is the power of being."[13] Non-being is conquered by being even though being presupposes non-being. To affirm being in all that is finite and to believe that being surpasses non-being is an act of courage or faith. All living things overcome non-being; the creative person is the one who overcomes more non-being. God finally overcomes an infinite amount. As the ontological language is elaborated, it makes use of metaphor and symbol.

Power is expressed relationally. Life is dynamic, and power is expressed in the encounters of being whether in Sartre's glance between a person and another person or Toynbee's description of the encounters and struggles of history. Power is not exactly force or compulsion. It uses force and compulsion to move other beings, but force without limits would destroy the other beings and not be power but destruction.

Power, like love, reunites beings without destruction of the other. The reunion of others sometimes requires the use of force to protect love. Power to resist non-being to ensure the union is, as Luther recognized, the strange work of love. It may look like power politics, but if it is limited by justice, it may protect love. Love tries

[11] Friedrich Nietzsche: "Life Itself is to my mind the instinct for growth, for durability, for an accumulation of forces for power; where the will to power is lacking there is decline" in "The Anti-Christ," in *The Portable Nietzsche*, ed. Walter F. Kaufmann (New York: Viking Press, 1954), 572.

[12] Friedrich Nietzsche: "Life Itself is to my mind the instinct for growth, for durability, for an accumulation of forces for power; where the will to power is lacking there is decline" in "The Anti-Christ," in *The Portable Nietzsche*, ed. Walter F. Kaufmann (New York: Viking Press, 1954), 572.

[13] Tillich, *Love, Power, and Justice*, 37.

not to destroy one who is against love, but it may act to destroy him. Every person, like every society, is a balance of elements in relation to the decisions of the center. Tillich is willing to speak of self-control but not of self-love or self-power.

Social groups relate to each other through power encounters. Each group tries to grow or to preserve itself, and the competition is inevitable. The struggle is over both space (land) and vocational vision. Each power driving to expand expresses its sense of vocation. The book written in 1953 expressed the power struggles of the USA and USSR as vocational struggles rooted in their values as well as a struggle for domination. He could speak of a growing imperialism in the USA to express its vocation of capitalism and constitutional freedom for half the world and implicitly for the whole world.

On the question of the unity of humanity, he saw the dynamism of humanity preventing it. He hoped for a federation in Europe and could consider it for continental unions. Not expecting voluntary world reunion, he could see liberal-democratic domination of the world as a possibility for a time, but he did not expect it to endure if achieved. Since his time, the "minimal suppression" that an emerging world empire would require has been lost. Wars in Asia have made the potential domination of a liberal vocation less attractive. The element of violent force in US power has obscured the attraction of American justice rendering world order impossible on that basis. Tillich's vision of a mixture of imperial vocations and continental power encounters among nation states, empires, and corporations continuing seems likely. World politics remains national and imperial struggles limited somewhat by developing law and voluntary institutional relations and economic ties.

No world empire can win its way to world domination, and the competition among regional empires, Russia, China, the European Union, and the United States, will characterize the whole. Our reality in 2014 approximates the world suggested by Tillich in 1954. The symbol of the Kingdom of God is sometimes glimpsed as the unity of love, power, and justice. It remains a symbol of unity for many but not for the whole world. It remains for those a work of human imagination projected out of their current disunities.

SYSTEMATIC THEOLOGY

In *Systematic Theology*, vol. 1 (1951) God "is the power of being in everything and above everything, the infinite power of being."[14] The definition is for Tillich the first step in writing an adequate theology. God as the "power of being or being itself" is used consistently throughout volume 1. Power has a priority in the theology over love or justice it is constitutive of the meaning of ontology and God.

"God is the answer to the question of being,"[15] appears at the beginning of his constructive interpretation of the symbol of God, and it was preceded by the whole discussion of method and reason. Power as the power of being is central to everything Tillich writes theologically, and power, sociologically, is central to everything he writes sociologically.

The ontology of volume 1 is repeated briefly in volume 2 and underlies the healing power of those participating the "New Being," within the ambiguities of life.[16]

Systematic Theology, vol. 3 continues the same ontology on power.[17] The discussion is framed in terms of the purpose of life being the fulfillment of particular beings, but he recognized the impossibility of fulfillment under the conditions of existence. Ambiguity becomes an important category leaping from the titles of chapters and paragraphs of text. Many of the arguments from *Love, Power,*

---

[14] Paul Tillich, *Systematic Theology*, vol. 1 (Chicago: The University of Chicago Press, 1952), 236.

[15] Tillich, 163.

[16] Paul Tillich, *Systematic Theology*, vol. 2 (Chicago: The University of Chicago Press, 1957).

[17] Paul Tillich, *Systematic Theology*, vol. 3 (Chicago: The University of Chicago Press, 1963).

and Justice are repeated in volume 3, but now the ambiguity is more pronounced. The estrangement of historical life is entered into more deeply, I think, than in his previous writing. Probably part of this is age. He published it at 77 years of age, and at my 81st year I regard some of my causes as historical successes, but I am also aware of the incompleteness of those successes and of even more failures.

His new homeland participated in a vocational struggle with an alternate empire, producing a drive toward catastrophe, and the avoidance of disaster was never guaranteed. Now, after the Cold War, my homeland, relatively uninformed about Islam or its religious/political struggles, risks falling into a century of conflict between American religious militants and Islamic religious militants dragging in more moderate, tolerant groups.

In his version of Christian faith, power or its expressions in democracy or empire cannot be despised. But both must be guided by justice regulating this power and criticizing the appearance of power without community and balances of interests. Too often, both empire and democracy have been absolutized and thereby obscured signs of the promise and critique of the Kingdom of God. Tillich believed the creativity of human life will continue to produce diverse centers of power which will resist the unification of humanity. The Kingdom of God is both immanent and transcendent of history. It is real enough to be glimpsed in experience, and one can sacrifice for it to express meaning and to promise fulfillment.

A THEORY OF POWER

James Adams provided the title "Shadow and Substance: A Theory of Power" to the lecture Tillich gave at the Department of Agriculture in the year of his death. Tillich had mentioned five other suggested titles for the lecture. The lecture is definitely his final word on the subject as his own power waned.

His attitudes toward active politicians are positive and his work is to help them find the humane meaning in their work. Outside the lecture hall the Vietnam War was escalating, and much of his former nation is the outpost of the American armed empire. His own particular towns of origin were outposts of the Russian Empire in occupied Poland, and his city of Berlin was surrounded.

"Almighty God is the unconditioned power which characterizes God as God.[18] Power is essentially good. Human life is called the "image of God." It is the fullest expression of the existent power of being in its liberation from the soil and in humanity's capacity to destroy a large part of life on earth.

Social power lacks the personal center of a human life, but it is centered in government. The centers of social power are responsible for defense of the whole. However, the lines between defense and attack become blurred. Social power means centeredness expressing a will, having space, and the possibility of growth. Tillich brings justice close to love as love is understood as the will to unite the separated. The drive for union requires form, and this form is justice, which preserves the uniting parts. When this justice is creative justice and allows the uniting parts to be fulfilled, it expresses the love of Christian ethics.

But in reality, all is estranged. Love, justice, and power in human existence are all twisted and distorted. Life is ambiguous. The distortions in our families, societies, and international relations require coercion to support the real justice and love in the units from disintegrating. Coercion is ever present but tragic. The application of coercion deepens the human estrangements, and in human distortions we create enemies to justify our guilt over using coercion.

Churches founded in the surrender of power by Jesus may not undertake coercion either spiritually or forcefully. States, on the other hand, find meaning in coercion to hold themselves together. States can operate without hate, but not without defensive coercion

---

[18] Paul Tillich, "Shadow and Substance: A Theory of Power," in *Political Expectations,* ed. James Luther Adams (New York: Harper & Row Publishers, 1971), 116.

to maintain unity. He moved toward the inevitability of the use of force and urges that in each situation it be guided by the wisdom of love.

He concluded with a strong denial of the moral possibility of using nuclear weapons, because they would "contravene the divine wisdom and future possibilities of human history."[19] The lecture was only two years after the Cuban missile crisis and nuclear brinkmanship. Basically, he made the Just War Theory point that the goals of a war must be just and that was inconceivable for a nuclear war. He has moved away from US nuclear policy and judged it not by the situation strictly, but by a classical principle. He suggested that he had shown in the lecture that the use of power did not contravene Christian ethics. He recognized that love and power coexist, but they also conflict. He hoped for the union of love and power partially in history, but only fully in eternity.

By May of 1963 his friends were already resisting the American inheritance of the French colonial war in Vietnam. A word from him as to the futility of war without purpose given to force would have been appreciated. His creative call for resistance to nuclear weapons could have been matched by resistance to the Americanization of that Vietnam civil war.

[19] Tillich, 123.

Chapter 8

RELIGIOUS SOCIALIST AND LIBERATION PERSPECTIVES ON JUSTICE[1]

The religious socialism of Paul Tillich preceded liberation theology and consequently never entered into dialogue with it. Liberation theologians of Latin America do not know much about Tillich's religious socialism and have not engaged it in dialogue. This chapter is an attempt to bring into dialogue two traditions which themselves have engaged only meagerly in conversation.

The North American Paul Tillich Society has maintained some conversation with both parties to the dialogue. Even in its pre-founding days, when the Society existed as a consultation in the American Academy of Religion, attention was given to Tillich's social thought and its parallels to liberation theology. Several papers and published essays of the Society have either discussed parallels or

[1] This chapter was originally published in *Laval theologique et philosophique* 44, no. 2 (June 1988): 155-67, and it was published as "Religious Socialism and Liberation Theology" in Mary Ann Stenger and Ronald H. Stone, *Dialogues of Paul Tillich* (Macon: Mercer University Press, 2002), 188-203.

suggested that the discussion between the two movements would be fruitful.[2] Similarly, the Society of Christian Ethics had religious socialist members who were interested in both Tillich's social thought and in liberation theology.[3] Enthusiasts for Tillich are in many cases, but not all, interested in keeping the memory of his religious socialism alive. There are individuals scattered throughout the continents who understand their analysis of social reality in a mixture of liberation and religious socialist themes. In my mind's eye, I visualize a thin line of Tillich scholars around the world who still work out of Tillich's socialist convictions. In the United States, as distinct from much of the rest of the world, religious socialism is not very alive. However Americans observe a revival of democratic socialism within the Democratic and Democratic Socialist parties. My late friend, Dorothee Sölle, in a meeting of the religious-socialist working group of the American Academy of Religion a few years ago, referred to religious socialism in the United States as a discussion group "with neither a church nor a party."

The student of liberation theology will find only occasional references to Tillich in the literature. Rubem Alves' book *Protestantism and Repression* utilizes Tillich extensively in delineating his ideal type of Right-Doctrine-Protestantism to show the repressive tendencies

---

[2] John B. Lounibos, "Paul Tillich's Structures of Liberation," in *Tillich Studies, 1975*, ed. John J. Carey (Tallahassee: Florida State University, 1975): 63-74; H. Frederick Reisz, Jr., "Liberation Theology of Culture: A Tillichian Perspective" in *Kairos and Logos*, ed. John J. Carey (Cambridge: The North American Paul Tillich Society, 1978): 300-11; Theodore Runyon, "Tillich's Understanding of Revolution" in *Theonomy and Autonomy*, ed. John J. Carey (Macon: Mercer University Press, 1984), 267-80; James W. Champion, "Tillich and the Frankfurt School," *Soundings* 169, no. 4 (Winter 1986): 81-101.

[3] Dennis P. McCann, "Tillich's Religious Socialism: Creative Synthesis of Personal Statement?" in *The Thought of Paul Tillich*, eds. James Luther Adams, Wilhelm Pauck, and Roger Lincoln Shinn (San Francisco: Harper & Row Publishers, 1985).

of modern Protestantism.4 But he makes no use of the liberating possibilities of Tillich's religious socialism. Gustavo Gutiérrez has not referred to Tillich's religious socialism in writing. References to the German situation of the Nazi period in liberation theology are largely in terms of Bonhoeffer or the Confessing Church.

The comparison between Gustavo Gutiérrez's and Paul Tillich's religious socialism seemed appropriate. They share many common emphases. They both emphasize personal dimensions of religious life as expressed in mysticism and in human psychology. Marxism, class struggle, and social revolution or socialism are significant in their thought. They are concerned to maintain their respective traditions while participating in reforming those traditions. They both express the characteristics Erik Erikson assigned to the term *homo religiosii*. They agonized personally over the inadequacies of their received traditions and in articulating new visions of religion transformed the human consciousness of many people with a worldwide impact.

The two belong to a type of religious social thought. Comparison between the two is within a type, it cannot express the degree of dissonance that Tillich's work between Buddhism and Christianity exhibited.5 This examination of their social thought focuses on *justice* and *revolution* while touching on related concerns.

JUSTICE

Ismael Garcia's dissertation directed by James Gustafson was published as *Justice in Latin American Theology of Liberation*.6 The focus of the work is on Hugo Assmann, José Míguez Bonino, Gustavo

---

[4] Rubem A. Alves, *Protestantism and Repression: A Brazilian Case Study* (Maryknoll: Orbis Books, 1985).

[5] Paul Tillich, *Christianity and the Encounter of the World Religions* (New York: Columbia University Press, 1963).

[6] Ismael Garcia, *Justice in Latin American Theology of Liberation* (Atlanta: John Knox Press, 1987).

Gutiérrez, and José Porfirio Miranda. Gutiérrez is regarded as the classical figure of the movement and his work is consulted most regularly in the book. The first major chapter, entitled "The Centrality of Justice in Latin American Theology of Liberation," argues that justice is the central concern of liberation theology. However, he is forced to argue that though "social justice is central to the reflection and practice of liberation theologians, they never present a clear statement of what they mean by this frequently used term."[7]

The argument develops that any formal definition of justice would come from the needs of the poor. Warnings are given against the dangers of an ahistorical understanding of justice. Justice may not be defined abstractly. The author admits, even in the conclusion, that the authors of liberation theology remain unclear about the meaning of justice but that the elements necessary for a clear definition are available in their work. The elements may be there, but the process of clarifying the relationship of those elements would still be a pretty abstract piece of work. Or maybe they cannot be clarified without more analysis.

Throughout Garcia's book the term *liberation*, which is defined abstractly, dominated the term *justice*. The work of liberation theology is focused mostly on conceptual work for overthrowing injustice rather than the building work of justice. Justice certainly presupposes order and liberation theology could not advocate order in any Latin American country at the present. Hannah Arendt's distinction between the work of fighting for freedom and structuring freedom is relevant here. Garcia may have been led to focus on justice because of the necessary fight against injustice.

The conclusion discusses aspects of justice from a liberation perspective. They are as follows:

(1) Justice is based on each person's equality of worth.

---

[7] Garcia, 11.

(2) Justice reflects humanity's social nature.

(3) Justice is based on a criterion of need.

(4) Justice means eliminating all inequality.

(5) Institutions which care for the poor deserve support in a just society.

(6) Justice implies the rich nations helping the poor nations.

(7) Well-being has a priority over freedom given the historical struggles.

(8) In the Latin American context, only some form of socialism will lead to justice.

The perspective of Garcia is that "justice can only be properly defined in the activity of bringing it about in light of the concrete situations that limit its realization."[8] This passion for the liberation process motivates this study and allows Jacques Maritain and other theorists who used natural law theory to define justice to be set aside. The natural law theory produced understandings of justice which informed Christian Democratic parties' reform efforts. But when reform has been overcome, Garcia argues, the process called for is liberation. If socialist liberation is not on the foreseeable horizon for most of Latin America, we are called back to look at alternative definitions of justice. For many countries striving to creep out from under military government or aspiring to moderate one party government, some of the more traditional definitions of justice may still be helpful.

Lebacqz finds the contribution of Miranda and Gutiérrez to a theory of justice to be in their staying close to a Biblical meaning of

[8] Garcia, 120.

righteousness.[9] She explains that for Miranda and Gutiérrez justice is real, right relationships. This requires special attention to the poor, for their situation must be altered. Justice is seen by their denunciations of injustice, particularly the injustices done to the poor of Latin America. The world is characterized by injustice, and God's work is particularly the righting of the wrongs which oppress the poor.

The important contribution of Gutiérrez requires an understanding of the Peruvian context which his translated works do not provide. When, in 1990, Gonzalo Castillo-Cardenas and I visited him, the social research of his institute was published in Peru in *Paginas.* The Las Casas Center was located in Rimac, a poor suburb of Lima. Tillich suggested that the writings of socialism are unintelligible without a commitment to the social struggle reflected in socialism. Moreover, the writings of Gutiérrez are not intelligible without a commitment to solidarity with the poor to change their social situation. The poverty of Peru, which leads to starvation and exploitation, is the necessary context for understanding Gutiérrez's work. A remarkable book by Curt Cadorette is a necessary introduction to the Peruvian poverty of which Gutiérrez writes.[10] Cadorette makes clear to North American readers the context of the sharp contrast between the poverty of the poor Indians of Lima and the benefits of capitalism to the wealthy of Lima. Moreover, he puts context to the footnotes of Gutiérrez to the Peruvian thinkers upon whom Gutiérrez draws. For years Gutiérrez taught a course based on the ideas of Mariátegui of adapting Marxist analysis to a critical dialectical understanding of Peruvian society and religion.[11] Similarly, Gutiérrez's friendship with and utilization of the Peruvian social-

[9] Karen Lebacqz, *Six Theories of Justice* (Minneapolis: Augsburg Publishing House, 1986).

[10] Curt Cadorette, *From the Heart of the People: The Theology of Gustavo Gutiérrez* (Oak Park: Meyer-Stone Books, 1988).

[11] Cadorette, 76.

novelist José Maria Arguldas reveals the depth of the truth captured in the title of Gutiérrez's book *We Drink From Our Own Wells*. His work draws upon these Peruvian thinkers and current sociological-anthropological research, including the work of his own institute. His utilization of Marxist critiques of society was indigenous, drawing upon a long history of its critical application to the society of Peru. In the immediate context it had to take account of the new reality of Christian base communities in which he invested his life, the shifts in ecclesiastical politics, the realities of the threat from *Sendero Luminoso*, or Shining Path guerilla movement, the possibilities of the Alan Garcia regime, the ever-present threat of military coup, the major players of international business, and the intervention by outside governmental pressures. Given the fluidity of all of these realities, Gutiérrez's realism led to shifts in his emphasis while continuing to look for openings in the situation which could give his people, the poor, a chance to improve their situation. His writings on justice and revolution are within the perceptions of a radically unjust, repressive social situation.

Gutiérrez writes of "institutionalized injustice" following the frequent use of it at the Pueblo conference. One finds more references to institutionalized injustice in his writing than institutionalized justice. One of his clearest paragraphs on justice is that the proclamation of Jesus of the Kingdom of God is the proclaiming of a Kingdom of justice and liberation. Justice for him is absolute:

> The only justice is the one that assaults all the consequences and expressions of this cleavage in friendship. The only justice is the definitive justice that builds, starting right now, in our conflict-filled history, a kingdom in which God's love will be present and exploitation abolished.[12]

Justice is used to denounce the present as a perspective from

---

[12] Gustavo Gutiérrez, *The Power of the Poor in History: Selected Writings* (Maryknoll: Orbis Books, 1983), 14.

which all oppressors will be overthrown. Liberation or the overthrow of the structures dominates the writing, rather than justice as something that the rulers could now deliver.

In his meditations on Job, Gutiérrez makes it clear that though justice is essential to the meaning of God, the meaning of God is not circumscribed by any theories of justice. Job has been freed in the end from "the temptation of imprisoning God in a narrow conception of justice."[13] The theology of retribution is abandoned, but the obligation of doing justice with God is affirmed. We seem to lack in Gutiérrez that which Karen Lebacqz and Ismael Garcia were looking for, "a theory of justice."

Justice was not the central term of Paul Tillich's religious socialist polemic against capitalism. He did not often judge capitalism by the criteria of justice; rather, he assumed the contradictions within capitalism were going to destroy it. He regarded the spirit of capitalism as the proclamation of a self-sufficient finitude, and his basic argument with it was that it was not open to the experience of the Unconditioned. Capitalism encouraged alienation, competition, and meaninglessness, and it was self-destructive. Justice became a central concept for Tillich in his American experience when the socialist cause, or at least the expression of it in the categories of the young Marx, seemed irrelevant to the American social scene.

Three exceptions to the above generalization are his essays: "Grundlinen des Religiosen Sozialismus" (1923),[14] "Man and Society in Religious Socialism (1943),[15] and *The Socialist Decision*

---

[13] Gustavo Gutiérrez, *On Job* (Maryknoll: Orbis Books, 1987), 91.

[14] Paul Tillich, "Grundlinen des Religiosen Sozialismus," in *Blatter für Religiosen Sozialismus*, IV Heft 8/100 (1923). Also in *Political Expectation,* trans. and ed. James Luther Adams (New York: Harper & Row, Publishers, 1971), 58-88.

[15] Paul Tillich, "Man and Society in Religious Socialism," *Christianity and Society* 8, no. 4, (1943): 10-20.

(1933).[16] Neither the essays nor the book push the discussion of justice to the ontological depths of his later work. None of the works use the criteria of justice as a weapon by which to criticize society the way Reinhold Niebuhr did in the same period. It could further be said that the Hegelian background is just below the surface in the 1923 work, and the 1943 essay is more reminiscent of the political philosophical discussion in England and America.

According to the 1943 essay, human nature bears the claim that every human being be recognized as a person.[17] There is a natural equality which is the equality of claim to express one's creativity, later he would say power of being. "This is the ultimate criterion of justice."[18] Justice concedes to finitude that the contingent characteristics of human existence prevent absolute equality. But justice requires that all accidental differences, by which he meant sex, race, intelligence, strength, birth, ought not to infringe upon essential equality. Therefore, all the structures which reinforce *essential* inequality were to be opposed. Fascism, monopolistic capitalism, and class-determined education all result in dehumanization, or the violation of the opportunity to express one's power of being, and therefore they were opposed to justice.

Justice plays an important role in Tillich's most profound socialist writing. *The Socialist Decision* was written in 1932 under the pressures of reactionary seizure of power in Berlin by Chancellor Franz Von Papen and the romantic-revolutionary gains by the Nazis. In Tillich's analysis, neither party represented the claims of justice. They both appealed to myths of the origins of life and not to a future shaped by the critique of justice. Tillich argued for an understanding of socialism that would be religious in its respect for the origins of being and prophetic in its insistence on justice. The symbol of the future is "expectation." Expectation expresses the direction

[16] Paul Tillich, *The Socialist Decision*.
[17] Tillich, "Man and Society," 17.
[18] Tillich, 17.

of humanity; it is the power of human transformation. He finds the power of expectation in the longings of the proletariat to overcome the demonic condition under which they survive. In the book, the discussion of expectation is elaborately developed. It is a powerful precursor to the later theologies of hope. This development of expectation, which is a presentation of eschatology in secular-autonomous terms, obscures the importance of justice in the argument. Still, justice, though not elaborated, is central. The call of the future is that of justice. Justice is the demand arising in human consciousness that calls for the future to be different. Justice requires expectation. Tillich puts it, "The ought is the fulfillment of the is. Justice is the true power of being."[19]

Justice means "the dignity of being free, of being the bearer of the fulfillment implied in the origin. This recognition of the equal dignity of the 'Thou' and the 'I' is justice."[20] Here, though not stated, is the definition of justice as the second commandment of Jesus: "Love your neighbor as yourself." Similarly, to the religious reader the trusting in expectation for the proletariat is similar to really living as if one expected an answer in history to the daily prayer "Thy Kingdom come." Tillich's argument in the book depends upon the proletariat and the proletariat's ability to understand its possibilities of transforming its historical situation. The book is committed to the possibilities of the proletariat. Of course very few of the proletariat could have understood the book if they had read it. Nazi suppression of the book in 1933 made even an attempted reading of it impossible.

Beyond the justice rooted in I-Thou encounters, Tillich speaks of justice as the consent to the social contract. Justice is therefore necessary to power as distinct from force. Consent to power, in the long run, depends upon the recognition of justice.

---

[19] Tillich, *Socialist Decision*, 6.

[20] Tillich, 6.

> Consent is given because those who assent to the exercise of power consider the way in which the unified will is executed to be just. The exercise of power appears to be just when all members of a society can acknowledge that their own will is contained in the will of the whole.[21]

Tillich perhaps overestimated the need for assent to a successful party's version of justice by other groups. The Nazis demonstrated the power of terror and force in dissuading groups with alternative visions of justice from competing for power. Tillich's hope in linking justice to power was to dissuade socialists from utopian politics that neglected power. For him, "the problem of power proves to be the problem of a concrete justice."[22] In his perspective, the Social Democrats had failed to "exercise and consolidate" power when it had come to them. Socialism in his view had been stronger in working on elaborating justice than it had been in exercising power. The state depends upon both justice and power, and effective politics required an understanding of their mutual dependence. Justice for Tillich in this 1932 writing was the movement toward the classless society and the planned economy. It was antithetical both to the revolutionary Nazis and the reactionary Junkers. It depended upon the emergence of both a tougher and a more religious socialism. The failure of such a movement to emerge permitted the Nazis to win and consolidate power without justice and for barbarism to reign on a formerly Christian Europe.

Tillich's 1954 work *Love, Power and Justice* is his most systematic discussion of justice. Here he unites reflection on justice with two concepts on which he had worked for years, love and power. He attempted to find a way between cynics, who would reduce justice to the meaning of power, and idealists, who would assert the demands of justice without reference to power. He sought to overcome dichotomies in Protestant ethics between justice and love without

---

[21] Tillich, 139.
[22] Tillich, 141.

collapsing them into each other.

The method of the volume may be confusing.[23] I would regard the method as that of conceptual analysis of basic categories of ethics and politics. Tillich asserts that such elaboration is the work of ontology. Consequently, he calls what I would regard as conceptual analysis of terms that have ontological implications as well as other meanings, ontological analysis. Also much of the method is etymology, but Tillich, in his search for "root" meanings of terms, also regards this as ontology. This difference in naming the method Tillich uses does not vitiate the results for me. It does mean, however, that the following of Tillich's argument leaves the conclusions as to the relationship of love, power, and justice as one model reflecting several human, even political, decisions rather than seeing it as a conclusion necessarily rooted in the way things ultimately are. Tillich's Protestant principle forces him to agree with the above conclusion.

"Justice is the form in which the power of being actualizes itself."[24] All beings drive towards transcending themselves in Tillich's ontology. This drive toward transcendence produces competition, and justice is the form that allows creativity to be expressed without destroying the whole.

The principle of justice is: love which contains a) adequacy, b) equality, c) personality, and d) liberty. Community or fraternity was rejected as part of the formal definition of justice by Tillich, yet he rejects the arguments of those who refuse to include it. His noting of the issue seemed to slight the importance of the issue. Community is certainly more than "an emotional principle adding nothing essential to the rational concept of justice."[25] One could hope for more of a discussion of fraternity, which was so important in the French Revolution. He discusses community mostly under the

---

[23] See Alistair M. Macleod, *Paul Tillich: An Essay on the Role of Ontology in his Philosophical Theology* (London: George Allen & Unwin Ltd., 1973).

[24] Paul Tillich, *Love, Power, and Justice*, 56.

[25] Tillich, 62.

rubric of "Holy Community" whereas plain human community could have used more discussion. All through the discussion of the principles of justice, Tillich can be seen analyzing the concepts as they appeared historically, but also stipulating his preferred meanings. The stipulations reflect his existentialist background and his protest against dehumanization.

The principles of justice are applied at various levels of justice. He lists the: a) intrinsic, b) the tributive, including 1) distributive, 2) attributive, and 3) retributive, and c) transforming. The transforming level of justice is where the Biblical roots of Tillich's discussion of justice are most clear. Creative or transforming justice is the form of reuniting love which does what is necessary for the reunion of beings.

> Love does not do more than justice demands, but love is the ultimate principle of justice. Love reunites; justice preserves what is to be united. It is the form in which and through which love performs its work. Justice in its ultimate meaning is creative justice, and creative justice is the form of reuniting love.[26]

The background of Tillich's discussion of justice reaches through his entire thought, but perhaps enough has been said to provide a context for understanding his aim. The influence of Hegel is particularly strong in *Love, Power, and Justice,* and the fragment on love is particularly in the background. Tillich's oft repeated statement that the relationship between theology and politics was the driving force of Hegel's system applies only a little less accurately to Tillich.

Tillich recognized the need for a socialist ethic while promoting socialism, but he did not write it. Consequently, his term *justice* was underdeveloped in his most socialist period. Despite Garcia's claim for its centrality in liberation theology, it appears there to be subsumed under the categories of liberation. Only in the older Tillich

---

[26] Tillich, 71.

does it become a central term, and here it is expressed as the form which allows life to flourish and not as a denunciation of the present. Tillich's discussion of justice can be read from his earlier commitments of passionate, religious socialism, but the book itself is not written that way. The formal presentation of justice, which the liberation theologians avoided, seems to lose its force of moral indignation against the present in Tillich. In this book, particularly, the absence of the proletariat is felt. Tillich did not find a proletariat in America, and the force of his socialism was lost. He did not have the liberation special class of the poor. His groups are national groups, not classes, in this writing. Tillich does not expect fulfillment in history; Gutiérrez demands social fulfillment and righteousness. It may be just this passionate zeal for overthrowing structures of injustice that prevented Gutiérrez from presenting an adequate formal definition.

REVOLUTION

As a religious socialist Paul Tillich supported the revolution which ended the German Empire. He hoped that the revolution would both push the social changes in a socialist direction and become more consciously a religious movement. He tried, in the pre-Nazi period, to defend the humanistic gains of the revolution, and in 1932 he urged it to deepen its socialist commitments. If one regards the Nazi coup of 1933 as a revolution, Tillich participated in losing a revolution. His urging the defeat of National Socialism from 1933-1945 could be seen as counter-revolutionary struggle by a political exile, though I would rather regard his efforts as a continuation of the religious-socialist revolution which was never achieved.

In *Systematic Theology*, revolution is discussed as part of historical ambiguity in relationship to the Kingdom of God. Sentences recall his fight with Emmanuel Hirsch, e.g. "Demonic consequences result from absolutizing the fragmentary fulfillment of the aim of history."[27] Also, the discussions of personal bitterness and the disruption of human ties must refer to the conflicts with his friend turned enemy.[28] Other sentences are reminiscent of his own socialist revolutionary essay: "In such movements of expectation, however unrealistic they may be, the fighting Kingdom of God scores a victory against the power of complacency in its different sociological and psychological forms."[29] By the time of publication of this volume, Tillich has lived a long time with revolution (1918-1963), and he can neither deny the hopes of revolutionaries nor expect the fulfillment of those hopes. He remembers his own excesses and also the power of hope. There is no general solution. The status quo movements and churches need the spirit of transformation. The prophetic movements and churches need the reminder of the ambiguity of history and of individual fulfillment in the Kingdom of God.

Revolutions are sometimes the only way to release new creativity. They may be crushed in counter-revolution, and suppression may mean less creativity than before the struggle. Tillich rejected the anti-revolutionary bias of much of the tradition of the church while cautioning of the dangers of revolution.[30]

Gutiérrez regards theology of liberation as a style of reflection in solidarity with the poor who are struggling to abolish injustice. It is in alliance, often, with Marxists. Its goal is to assist in building a new society. In the new society, the ownership of the means of production will not be in private nor foreign hands. Obviously, in *A Theology of Liberation* a revolution overthrowing the present rulers was a goal. The theology itself will be verified "by active, effective participation in the struggle which the exploited social classes have

---

[27] Tillich, *Systematic*, vol. 3, 390.

[28] Tillich, 343-44.

[29] Tillich, 391.

[30] Tillich, 388-89.

undertaken against their oppressors."[31] Gutiérrez's early writing is clear enough to be understood as advocating the church changing sides, raising consciousness, and forming a critical-supportive theology of revolution by the poor. Often, his own perspective is hidden in his exegesis of the revolutionary potential of the documents of Medellion and Pueblo which he had a hand in writing. His advocacy of social revolution is clearest in the section "Towards a Transformation of the Latin American Reality."[32]

By the time *A Theology of Liberation* was published in English, his writing in Spanish eliminated any doubt as to his meaning.[33] The poor were being heard but only by those engaged in the revolutionary struggle against the Latin American order. The poor were to end the class society, appropriate the means of production, undertake their own political order, and engage in the creation of a new consciousness.[34] The coming into the revolutionary practice he described as "the *most important fact* in the life of the Latin American Christian community."[35] Admitting some dependence on the theologies of revolution, Gutiérrez distinguishes the popular movements from such theologies. For here in the popular movements the thinking is by the people within the struggle rather than it being thought outside and applied to the struggle. This distinction is not easily grasped, but it does, I believe, point to a distinction between Gutiérrez's theology of transformation and Tillich's philosophy of transformation.

Gutiérrez really is more of the people than Tillich ever was of

---

[31] Gustavo Gutiérrez, *A Theology of Liberation*, 15th anniversary edition (Maryknoll: Orbis Books, 1988), 174.

[32] Gutiérrez, 63-68.

[33] Gutiérrez, *Power of the Poor in History*, 37. Book first published in 1973 in Spanish.

[34] Gutiérrez, 37-38. It is probable that this description of the goals of the revolutionary society is Gutiérrez's meaning of justice.

[35] Gutiérrez, *38.*

the proletariat. Tillich's early ministry was with the proletariat, but his life was with the intellectuals after World War I. Gutiérrez's research and much of his teaching is with the poor. Of course, the programs of both were dependent on the potency of the class for which they articulated socialism. Tillich's proletariat seemed to disappear in post-war America. Gutiérrez's poor seem unlikely to disappear in Latin America. Given the immediacy of the suffering, and the program of revolution, we need only to see if Gutiérrez maintains any of Tillich's sense of ambiguity about revolution. The ambiguity is not present in his early writing. The task of liberation theology was to assist Christians into the Latin American revolutionary process.[36]

In his later writing, however, the theme of joining the revolutionary process is muted. Obviously, he could not urge Christians to join the Shining Path, which led a revolutionary struggle in his own country. When I visited him at his Institute, the Church had already suppressed him and limited his movement. The national security states have destroyed revolutionary movements throughout Latin America. A sadder, more contemplative Gutiérrez is read in his lectures in Peru in 1982, *We Drink from Our Own Wells*.[37] The mystic, non-activist writer Henri Nouwen wrote the introduction and seemed to value the spiritual crisis of Central America as "something more than political conflict."

The turn toward spirituality was a possible development from *A Theology of Liberation*. It was only one possible development; he could have developed in terms of social ethics or deeper social analysis. But many have been killed, and his writing reflects their martyrdoms, though he does not reflect on Che Guevara and Camilo Torres as he did in his earlier work. My late colleague Gonzalo Castillo spoke of a Gutiérrez evolving out of his emphasis on social

---

[36] Gutiérrez, 173.

[37] Gustavo Gutiérrez, *We Drink from Our Own Wells: The Spiritual Journey of a People* (Maryknoll: Orbis Books, 1984).

revolution. Perhaps such an evolution is necessary as revolution in a socialist direction is not imminent and the persecution is terrible. The most recent book of meditations, *On Job*, has also dropped the theme of social revolution. There were cold winds of repression blowing from the Vatican. The papacy of Francis may be more moderate. Finally, if the theology of liberation is to truly be the second act, it must wait for social revolution in South America to mature before it can reflect upon it. He wrestles with Job, finding there an innocent suffering but a book still calling one to join God in struggling for justice. The choice of Job rather than Exodus for commentary is significant, however. When he writes here of his Peruvian context, he writes of the incredible suffering, deprivation, terrorism, and oppression. Then he writes: "What we must deal with is not the past, but, unfortunately, a cruel present and a dark tunnel with no apparent end."[38]

Themes of *kairos* and utopia are still present in Gutiérrez's writing, but they are muted. *Kairos* refers to a favorable time,[39] but the moment is of the Lord's knocking on the doors of the Latin American church community calling to solidarity, prayer, and deeper spirituality with the poor. The theme of utopia is still of a people building a new world, but the denunciation is more sorrowful than it was a decade earlier. The annunciation is not so clear. "The process is only beginning."[40]

The muted nature of these once powerful themes is familiar to students of Tillich. *Kairos* and utopia, in Gutiérrez, both required the transformation of the condition of the poor. Likewise, in Tillich, the connection between the proletariat and socialism saved socialism from utopianism. Only through the transformation of the proletariat could socialism arise. In his later years, the waiting expectantly in the sacred void while fighting evil replaced the expectation of the

[38] Gutiérrez, *On Job*, 102.
[39] Gutiérrez, *Our Own Wells*, 136.
[40] Gutiérrez, 27.

transformation of the proletariat. *The Socialist Decision* and *A Theology of Liberation* are both affirmative of utopian politics even though Tillich avoids the term. His later affirming of the "spirit of utopia," while avoiding utopianism, is more cautious. The religious socialism of the two remains much less demanding in their later years. In both cases it has been brutalized and defeated, in Tillich's case by National Socialism and, for the present, in Gutiérrez's case by the national security state in Chile, by terrorism and murder in other states, by the failures of socialism in Venezuela and Nicaragua, and by the dynamics of Peru.

The complexity and the richness of the minds of the two thinkers also contributed to their changing emphases. The frustration of religious socialism in Tillich's case freed him to evolve with more emphasis on psychology and religion and to write his *Systematic Theology*. In the case of Gutiérrez, his more recent writings and speeches are emphasizing spirituality and ecclesiology. The Marxist analysis has faded and his solidarity between the poor and a renewed church is within the bounds of approved Vatican social teaching.

Still, Gustavo's journey goes on.[41] God willing, new insights from the poor of Lima will be fertilizing his mind. The fading of Marxist categories may lead to a more thoroughly indigenous, more thoroughly Christian, social philosophy.

The accounts of both Gustavo and Paulus reveal dynamic thinkers taking account of their times. Both agreed that discussion of religious socialism required sensitivity to the struggle of the under classes, though they focus on different classes as the bearers of their hopes. Both revealed possibilities in a humane Marxism far removed from a dogmatic reading of Karl Marx or the cruelties of pre-Gorbachev

[41] Robert McAfee Brown concludes his short biography of Gutiérrez with a chapter "There Is No Conclusion: the Curtain Stays Up, the Play Goes On and We Are on Stage." *Gustavo Gutiérrez* (Atlanta: John Knox Press, 1980). My use of his first name in this paragraph is deliberate; it expresses our friendship and sense of comradeship in hope and faith.

Russian socialism. Both of them require socialism to be open to full religious expression of the people. Both of them are indigenous, we may say, existentialist thinkers. Together they reveal different forms of Christian-oriented reforms of society which the world needs for its health. Christian social philosophy has possibilities for assisting the poor in their struggles and also for the promotion of peace among the more affluent. I hosted Gutiérrez twice in Pittsburgh and visited him in Peru, and the social situation and political dynamics in both countries have darkened since our first meeting in 1976 to celebrate the American Revolution.

The Christian social philosophies of both thinkers were overcome by revolutionary developments. Tillich was driven into exile by the revolutionary Nazis. The World War II victories of the market-oriented democracies of the West and the Communism of the Soviet Union crushed hopes for religious socialism. The counter-revolutionary forces of the Vatican and the United States thwarted liberation theology's political aspirations and sometimes killed its practitioners. But it was the nonviolent revolutions of Eastern Europe and Russia in the late 1980s and early 1990s that really ended socialism and left market-oriented economies as the victors. Most of Latin America rushed to market-oriented reforms, abandoning state-planned or run economic corporations.

So, given the dominance of mixed-economy market driven systems, where is Christian social philosophy to turn? It seems that the reform-oriented action philosophies of a Tillich or a Gutiérrez have their heirs still in the parties of the left in Latin America, the socialists in France, Social Democrats in Germany, Labor party in Great Britain, liberals in the Democratic Party in the US, and social action departments and activists in the churches. Their commitments will be to emphasize the religious dimensions of depth and justice against the faces of secularism and capitalist greed. The struggle will continue to be to humanize the social organization of the world in the name of God. For the present, reform, not revolution, is the primary Christian social goal.

Chapter 9

TILLICH'S *KAIROS* AND ITS TRAJECTORY[1]

Paul Tillich's *Systematic Theology*, vol. 3, published in 1963, should be taken as his definitive word on the concept of *kairos*.[2] He asserts that since he used the term in his socialist writings the term has taken on a life of its own. It has been used and misused. It has been used demonically as well as creatively. Noting that it is more dependent on vision than science, in his own use he wants to subject possible uses of *kairos* to the "great" *kairos* of eternity meeting time in its New Testament context.[3] Other claims for the right time can be judged by the meaning of the coming of Christ. In the *Systematic Theology* it is the breakthrough of the Kingdom of God. Long before the final system was organized the term had become decisive for Tillich's presentation of religious socialism.[4] Paul Tillich's intimate

---

[1] This chapter is published simultaneously in Thomas Bandy, ed., *Why Tillich? Why Now?* (Macon: Mercer University Press, 2021)

[2] Tillich, *Systematic*, vol. 3, 369.

[3] Tillich, 369.

[4] See Ronald H. Stone, *Paul Tillich's Radical Social Thought* (Atlanta: John Knox Press, 1980).

discussion group in Berlin after World War I came to bear the name of the Kairos Circle. The term has continued through history to be affirmed by circles of Christian believers and their allies who have wanted to radically change societies. Within the Kairos Circle it was a resolution to the debate between activists and determinists who insisted that history would carry its own solutions forward. Action was needed, but it had to be in tune with the properties of the contemporary history which were open to radical change. Theologically, Tillich meant the term to bear the weight of the intersection of eternity and historical action. For him, history was ripe for the fulfillment of the ideas of the religious socialists. By 1932, he understood religion would have to radically change to be open to socialism, and socialism would have to radically change to be open to the ultimate claims of religion.

In Berlin in 1951, he would say that the religious socialist ideas of the interwar period were basically correct. He expressed the *kairos* as the Kingdom of God which was both transcendent and historical. In history, the Kingdom of God was only fragmentarily present. He thought the Kingdom of God concept pointed to fulfillment only in its vertical dimension. Still, it encouraged historical action in its immanent dimensions. In his personal opinion, the *kairos* lay ahead only in the distant future. He was speaking in Germany under Allied and Russian occupation. But in decolonization and the civil rights movement elsewhere in the world, moments of *kairos* were producing significant breakthroughs in mixtures of social revolution, religion, and liberalism. Maybe the 1922 statement was more utopian than he admitted. The 1951 statement was unnecessarily confined to the context of the Cold War, but as he said in the *Systematic Theology*, the concept had its own trajectory. The term was partly, and only partly, confirmed in the period of its emergence. His definition was: "Its original meaning—the right time, the time in which something can be done—must be contrasted with chronos, measured or clock time. The former is qualitative, the later quantitative."[5] He argues that its use in the *New Testament* shows it to reveal the maturity of time in which the Kingdom of God may manifest itself. But he notes the power to resist the Kingdom can also be magnified at the same time. He correctly notes the Biblical attribution of the term to both Jesus and Paul and mistakenly to John the Baptist.[6] He noted the term had other Greek uses than the *New Testament* use, and he did not enter into any particular exegesis of the term. Matthew Lon Weaver has investigated different connotations to the term in the *New Testament* and noted its rare uses in the *Septuagint*.7 Weaver noted how Tillich was partially wrong in his expectations of *kairos*, and he believed Tillich attached positive moral meaning to the term which it did not deserve. Tillich was careful in the *Systematic Theology* to note the concept was used destructively, and in sentences reminiscent of his quarrel with Emmanuel Hirsch he mentioned the demonic distortion of the idea by the Nazis. The apprehension of *kairos* is in vision and involves risk, as one or a group may be mistaken. An examination of the trajectory of the concept risks judgments on whether a group was correct in perceiving the *kairos* or not. For Tillich, a correct perception required correlation to the reality of Christ in Jesus, including the willingness to sacrifice the self for the cause. Prideful, self-serving movements could not be expressing an authentic *kairos*. Finally, he said the true *kairos* is unique and the *kairoi*, or lesser expressions of historical fulfillment, are rare. History usually proceeds with only glimpses of *kairos*. Contemporary use of the term different than Tillich's includes the singers from The Holy Cross Monastery, a young adult retreat center, many different prison

[5] Tillich, *Systematic*, vol. 3, 369.

[6] Tillich, 369.

[7] He categorizes eighty-eight uses of the term in the *New Testament* and finds fifty-five illustrations relevant to Tillich's use of the term. Matthew Lon Weaver, *Religious Internationalism: War and Peace in the Thought of Paul Tillich* (Macon: Mercer University Press, 2010), 289.

ministries, a publishing house, a Canadian relief agency of the churches, a technical agency, and studies in rhetoric which find the term being used by various Greek authorities including Protagoras and Hippocrates. An alternative connotation of the term is associated with *Kairos*, the youngest of Zeus' offspring and the god of opportunity. This apparently led to financial firms taking the title. The inquiry of these reflections focuses on eight theological groups encouraging social/political action fit to the times. Several organizations engaged in various excellent social service ministries are therefore not reported on in this confining of the term to groups seeking fundamental social change.

KAIROS AND PEACEMAKING

The Presbyterian General Assembly may have been the earliest church body to pick up the symbol and make it part of its official teaching. In 1980, in a period of national discouragement over the retreat from Vietnam, Russian assertiveness, the revolution in Iran, and economic stagnation, this church saw an opportunity for a new emphasis on peacemaking. It launched a program of peacemaking, sponsored an all church special offering to support it, hired several staff to work on the issues to change the consciousness of the church, to equip its members to engage in peacemaking, and to witness for peace to the nation. Its founding policy, *Peacemaking: The Believer's Calling*, requested Presbyterians to claim their vocations as peacemakers and declared peacemaking as a priority for the church.[8] Significant votes in local churches chose to support the program and the offering, and about one-third of approximately eleven thousand congregations chose to support the new effort. The language of *kairos* was used three times in the document to assert that this was

[8] The United Presbyterian Church in the U.S.A., *Peacemaking: The Believer's Calling* (Louisville: Office of the General Assembly, United Presbyterian Church in the U.S.A., 1980).

the time for the church to act decisively with new thinking, a budget, and bold actions.

The nation thought otherwise, and it entered into a period of arms buildup and assertive militancy under the Reagan Administration. The Presbyterian Head of Chaplains resigned his military office believing the Administration was preparing to fight a nuclear war rather than deter one. The church opposed the Administration's wars in Central America. The church considered declaring itself a resistance community against militarism, but in 1988 it instead opted to encourage extraordinary efforts with ordinary means to practice peacemaking. Gradually, the peacemaking program declined, and it shared its financial resources with other aspects of the church's mission. Though *kairos* became an important symbol in the church's theology, the church probably misjudged the times in 1980, and neither the times nor the church tasted the proclaimed *kairos*. The failure of the Peacemaking Program to keep alive the spirit of peacemaking as a sign of the *kairos* accompanied the general decline and splintering of the Presbyterian Church (USA).

SOUTH AFRICAN *KAIROS*

Kairos is more central in the *Kairos Document* of South Africa than it was in the Presbyterian document.9 In the 1986 edition it is defined as: "Kairos is the Greek word used in the Bible to designate a special moment of time when God visits his people to offer them a unique opportunity for repentance and conversion for change and decisive action."[10] The nation was in crisis and many were being killed in the movement to end apartheid. The document was drafted in a theological center, referred to many groups for amendment, published, criticized, and then, in 1986, republished in a second

[9] "The *Kairos Document*: Challenge to the Church," in *Kairos: Three Prophetic Challenges to the Church*, ed. Robert McAfee Brown (Grand Rapids: Wm. B. Eerdmans, 1990), 26.

[10] Brown, 95.

edition. It recognized the divisions in the country and within the church. It criticized the theologies of state and church then dominant in the country and called for a prophetic theology that was very specific as to the social diagnosis of apartheid and then offered methods for Christian action against apartheid. Arguing that God sides with the oppressed and wants to liberate the people the document called for participating in the struggle, transforming regular church activities into social change, the initiation of special campaigns against the apartheid system in churches, activities of civil disobedience against tyrannical government, and the provision of moral guidance, including counseling the liberators against those who would act "thoughtlessly and wildly."

The prophetic theology was articulated in terms of classical reformed arguments against tyranny. A government which acts against the common good which it is to serve is no government and needs to be replaced with a just government. The document recognized that the majority of Christians in the country were oppressed by the apartheid ideology and government and had already chosen to replace it. It set itself against the theology of both the apartheid ideology and the temporizing opposition to apartheid in the English churches. In this case the church participation in the struggle deepened, and within five years change came to South Africa and the theological contribution in this predominantly Christian nation was recognized. The document also helped Christians abroad think through the situation in South Africa and assist in supporting the struggle through divestment activities, boycotts, and civil disobedience.

KAIROS CENTRAL AMERICA

The Kairos Central American document of 1988 evolved through a process in which hundreds reviewed the document in the midst of civil wars. It was a time of the height of liberation theology, and the document expressed many of its themes. The sensitive reader picks up more Marxist themes than in the South African one, and, to that degree, it is closer to the language of Tillich's circle than its predecessors. The American empire is the enemy which allies with the church and the establishment to keep the poor in their exploited position. Jesus, the prophets, and Mary, who identify with the suffering of the poor, are called into service as enemies of the empire. God's Kingdom, a utopia, is to be built on earth by the exploited masses of Central America, and the process is seen in the success of the Sandinista movement in Nicaragua. The exploitation began with the Spanish conquest, and resistance against it has occurred for 500 years. But now in the present, opposition to the evil of the establishment is rising and can succeed in restoring peace and justice to Central America. Readers of the document are asked to take sides in the struggle with the poor to overthrow the rulers. The hour is seen as decisive by the writers. More than two hundred thousand had been killed in the previous ten years of struggle, and the writers believed history was coming to a climax. "This historic hour in Central America is a *kairos*, the passing of God incarnate in Jesus through the burning waste of Central America, calling us to fight for the Kingdom, to the cross, to unwavering hope, to invincible unity, to resurrection triumph.[11]

The appeals of the theologians assisting in the revolutions were heard abroad during the Cold War. In a peacemaking presentation in the University of Berlin I met theologians who were studying Spanish to better grasp liberation theology and who on the German-Poland border presented me with Nicaraguan coffee in 1983. But when I asked Bernard Häring in the Vatican how many were studying liberation theology there, he replied two, me and one of my students. The Vatican, with its campaign to free Poland, was not about to support any leftist revolutionaries against the United States in Central America. The Reagan Administration thought it was

[11] Brown, *Kairos*, 95.

fighting the Cold War there and not that it was aligning against a genuine long-standing revolution of the poor. The document dismissed the overreaction from the United States, but it was real and, to a degree, as determinative as the opposition of the Catholic Church or the Latin American establishment. The fall of the USSR had negative consequences for the liberation movements in Latin America. As the Vatican encouraged the hardening of the hierarchy against liberation theology, the local authorities often responded to discredit the movement. Even within Peru, Father Gustavo Gutiérrez's movements were limited. I agree the revolutionaries found a moment of personal and communal *kairos,* but the progressives were up against fierce opposition which they named as anti-kingdom forces. For the most part, the establishment won the battles, leaving a progressive remnant to work in more modest ways for the future, but hopes for radical change were defeated. Before the fall of the Soviet Union, decision makers in the US were pushed to extreme measures. Congress tried to shut down support for overthrowing the Sandinista government. President Reagan and his cohorts attempted to supply the Contras through the Iran-Contra deal discrediting their foreign policy and proving several of them guilty of illegal acts. The denial of the humanity of the poor continued. Later, the original revolutionaries would lose an election. Their return to power was very disappointing to the disaffected in Nicaragua by 2019. However, the governments surrounding it failed to alleviate poverty also. Refugees fleeing Central America precipitated a crisis for the Trump Administration and remained an election issue for the US in 2020. My colleague, the late Gonzalo Castillo-Cardenas, and I toured Latin American liberation projects in 1990 from Nicaragua to Chile. A few years ago, reflecting on the Central American experience, he suggested: "Our hopes for change were too high.

There has been little improvement in the condition of the poor."[12]

While Robert McAfee Brown saw similarities to the Barmen Declaration in these theologies, I see more cultural analysis characteristic of Tillich. The analysis is more from the church than Tillich's use of *kairos*, and the church is called to action in a way that Tillich could only have hoped for. However, the wider and more dramatic social critique is much more characteristic of Tillich than of Barth. The Barmen Declaration, for all of its power, was mostly confined to arguments for the freedom of the church to follow only Christ.[13] Brown began his story of *kairos* with Tillich, and then in an ending challenging the North American churches included the Barmen Declaration in the book.

KAIROS AND CHURCH STRUGGLE: TWO DOCUMENTS

Two church documents take the struggle straight to the church while not neglecting the social and historical context. *The Road to Damascus, Kairos and Conversion* was published deliberately on the tenth anniversary of the Sandinista victory in Nicaragua, July 19, 1989. It represented the reflection of hundreds of people in Africa, Central America, and Asia. It is framed in terms of liberation theology, and thousands indicated by signing that it reflected their will. It focused on the conflict between the left wing and the right within the Christian community. That conflict, resulting in oppression and murder, is the *kairos* of which the document speaks. The theme of Paul's conversion from a persecutor to an apostle on the Damascus road carries the proclamation on into the conflict within the communities of the church. The church's absorption into the Empire is

[12] Gonzalo Castillo-Cardenas, phone conversation with author, April 4, 2011.

[13] See Matthew Lon Weaver, "Theology of Resistance in Bonhoeffer and Barth," in *Resistance and Theological Ethics*, eds. Robert L. Stivers and Ronald H. Stone (Lanham: Rowman and Littlefield, 2004), 209-312.

regarded as apostasy leading to idolatry, and right wing Christianity is denounced as heretical. "Those Christians who side with the imperialists, the oppressors and the exploiters of people are siding with the idolaters who worship power, money, privilege and pleasure."[14]

Kairos Europa flowed from the Ecumenical Assembly of European churches in Basel in 1989. It is a movement interpreted as attempting to gather the churches in a *Status Confessionis* against neoliberal economics and its consequences. Ulrich Duchrow models his remarks after the Barmen Confession and treats neoliberal economic practice in national economics, the World Bank, and the International Monetary Fund as similar to Nazism and apartheid of the twentieth century even though its consequences of death and exclusion are more indirect.

The churches are called to redirect their investments and property to serve ecological and social welfare causes and away from banks and other institutions supporting capitalist globalization. A socially responsible economy is sought, which practices ecological responsibility. The movement calls for combating monetary policy and privatization. The World Alliance of Reformed Churches, in its organization, has developed many studies around confession and economics and finds the means of confession palatable to many of its leaders. Resistance to the trend is high among Reformed Christians in the US placing more trust in the market mechanisms of the economy and its host of international institutions. The *Kairos Europa* tends toward the sharpness of *The Road to Damascus Document* but with more of an emphasis upon economic theory. Earlier attempts to move toward a *Status Confessionis* against neoliberal economic trends have been led by Czech theologians more sympathetic to socialism than the reformed populations of the United States. Tillich's Kairos Circle concentrated less upon international economics, but the economic directions of that circle are distinctly echoed

[14] Brown, *Kairos,* 137.

in this form of *Kairos* document. The author admits to less direct involvement with these two documents than the previous three and turns toward the *Kairos Palestine* document "*A Moment of Truth*." The publication of the document and conversations with two of the authors inspired this paper.

PALESTINIAN *KAIROS*

The 2009 call to faith and action by the writers of *Kairos Palestine* honors the model of the South African document and study of Palestine. My visitations and study of Palestine since 1980 contribute to my support of their reading of the acts on the ground. They are occupied, subjected to apartheid like oppression, humiliated, and impoverished. Like the North American Native Americans, their land has been taken, their homes and crops destroyed, and they have been confined to reserves, where they are dependent upon welfare from others for their survival. The writers of the document do not see signs of immediate or near time relief. They fear they may be close to losing hope for their own state despite the world's clamor that their rights be recognized. For them, the *kairos* is a moment to speak, to tell the truth, and as they say: "Kairos is the moment when we see God's gifts in the midst of our suffering."[15]

The document is less on economics than on political theology. It lacks the socialist tendencies of the previous three documents. Rather, it is asking for the use of capitalist or mixed-economy means of boycott, divestment, and sanctions to dislodge Israel from its occupation. To this extent it is quite different from the political-economic theology of the original Kairos Circle, yet it continues the focus on time.

As Tillich became a supporter of Zionism, he shifted from the Time interpretation of Israel to the Space and Time interpretation,

---

[15] *Kairos Palestine: A Moment of Truth*, 2010, https://www.kairospalestine.ps/index.php/about-kairos/kairos-palestine-document, 4.

so this document is pushing for a Space-Time perspective. Jerusalem, or Al-Quds, is central to the document, and it is claimed as the future capital of Palestine. I read a paper on the pro-Zionism of Paul Tillich and Reinhold Niebuhr to a Christian audience including Arab scholars at Tantur, between Jerusalem and Bethlehem, in 1980. As the 2009 Christian document asserts, their perspective was that the sins of Europe should not have been repented of at the expense of the Arabs, as I was informed at the time. The issue is the land, and as an old Sioux chief in Iowa said in the previous century before he was murdered: "The white man wants all of the land."[16] To the Palestinian farmers, shepherds, and olive grove workers that I have visited, that is the issue here. In the United Nations only the United States of America supports Israel's expansion of its control of land and water of Palestine.

Beyond the facts of Israel's occupation and expansion on the ground, the document moves to its theology. It presents a Palestinian interpretation of faith, hope, and love as its foundation. Biblical criticism is utilized and fundamentalism rejected.

While theological themes are discussed, the idea that political policy could be read directly out of scripture is rejected. The Bible must be interpreted in a living way and in accordance with the rejection of repression, slavery, and the domination of one people over another. The document seems to me to be less utopian than some of the predecessor documents, and if in their enthusiasm for political change they slipped into romanticism, this document avoids those illusions. It is most Tillichian in its use of love, power, and justice, though it does not use Tillich's ontology at this point. Its tone is that of the mature Christian realist Tillich who demanded political change, perhaps in a tone like his denunciation of Hitler in 1933 or Senator Goldwater in 1964. It is most unlike Tillich in its rejection of Zionism and avoidance of socialist terminology. The occupation

[16] This quote is a family memory from a pioneer great-grandfather.

is denounced as sin. Resistance to oppression is to be carried out under the ethic of love. Such an ethic based in an understanding of Jesus must reject fighting evil with evil, but hue to nonviolent resistance. The history of resistance includes defending their own land through Israel's courts. Political petitions are reissued. They endure beatings and rebuild their homes after they are destroyed. I have eaten in homes destroyed by Israel four times and in tents removed regularly and reestablished. To hold on to their land they have built caves when home rebuilding is forbidden. Then the caves are trashed by the occupiers. Their resistance includes civil disobedience, and I have joined with other Christians, Jews, and Moslem demonstrators in actions. Resistance has included violence as a response to violence, but the writers and signers of the document reject the evil of violence and call for nonviolent suffering. Their major call for solidarity from the world churches is a request that they come on pilgrimage to Palestine. The writers pledge to show them the reality of Palestine while they pray with them. Sabeel has developed its own liturgies for such pilgrimages but adjusts them to the needs of visiting groups. They also ask churches to join with Palestinian Christians in supporting boycotts, divestment, and sanctions against the occupation (BDS). While rejecting the concepts of religiously based states, they pledge to work with their enemies and allies to build states for all, based in justice and civil liberties. The debate between the two or one state policy continues. While there are articulate Palestinian voices for the one state solution as Israel's aggression with US support seems invincible, this would be a reluctant recognition of reality. The preferred outcome would be two states with Jerusalem divided or internationalized, refugees repatriated or compensated, and the 1967 boundaries restored. The language of reconciliation and forgiveness in the document seems consistent with the character of the writers I know who are listed in the document. The statement is prophetic, and in its denunciations and strategies have been endorsed by heads of many of the churches in Palestine. It is part of the struggle within North American Protestantism to begin the divestment from American corporations that support the occupation, which is against international law. Israeli and Jewish denunciations of the *Kairos Palestine* are frequent, and they are available on the internet under *Kairos Palestine*. The support of this work by major Protestant denominations remains ambiguous with debates still going on within their ruling bodies. Some divestment has occurred, and resolutions critical of US foreign policy have been taken. In general the more fundamentalist/evangelical churches continue to support Israel's occupation, and the more mainline churches are critical of US economic policy regarding Palestine.

KAIROS: UNION THEOLOGICAL SEMINARY

The most recent institutional expression of *kairos* theological action has been at Union Theological Seminary.[17] The Seminary which provided a home for the political refugee Tillich in 1932 launched the Kairos Center in 2013 drawing upon Union's Poverty Initiative Mission Project for its own major program. The Kairos Center threw itself into the Poor People's Campaign, which renewed the heritage of the campaign planned by Martin Luther King, Jr. before his assassination in 1968. This current campaign, led by Dr. William Barber and Dr. Liz Theoharis of the Center, with Union's support, is organizing across the country to renew moral leadership in politics with a focus on poverty. The initiative involves the publication of research on removing poverty and on the training of leadership to help the poor lead the campaign which across the country resulted in many actions and resulted in arrests in Washington, D.C. and state capitols. As a visitor to the Poor People's tent city in Washington, D.C. in 1968, its sagging tents dripping in the rain were signs of the country's indifference to the poor after the murder of Martin

[17] Guthrie Graves-Fitzsimmons, "Igniting a Moral Revival," *Union Collective* (New York: Union Theological Seminary, Fall 2018): 8-13.

Luther King, Jr. This revival promises the best of Martin Luther King, Jr. and James Cone's liberation theology at Union and in the streets. The reports on the Center emphasize the joining of theological scholarship to action, embodying the best of the young Tillich. From those actions and his ecumenical colleagues, Jewish and Christian, came the concept of *kairos* with its call for action in political-economic terms.

CONCLUSION

Tillich was correct in *Systematic Theology*, vol. 3 that the *kairos* theology has its own life. Political, economic, theological, and ideological elements are all involved in social change, as are nonviolent and violent means of change. The Palestinian document inspired these reflections, but as it recognized, the *kairos* is not immediate, and it differs from the more socialist documents in being less involved in economic analysis. On the other hand, the *kairos* as eternal meaning intersecting the present is certainly evident in the Arabic-speaking world. Palestine may not be immune to change in ways not perceived by the authors of the Palestinian document. Religion and socialism are reconciled in many places, and Tillich's early theology is relevant, but it must be remembered it was pre-New Deal. New developments of it may become more relevant under social-welfare, mixed-market economies. Maybe the Union Seminary movement is a test of that possibility. Likewise *The Road to Damascus: Kairos and Conversion* and *Kairos Europa* are recognized more as critical utopias than as immediate historical projects. *Kairos Central America* was defeated by state and church, but the poverty and suffering of Latin America still cry out for revolutionary change and may provoke misguided interventions from the US. Many theologians and priests who supported the Sandinista Revolution in Nicaragua saw their dreams thwarted by the Ortega regime. The hope of countering American militarism has been eclipsed by militarism, economic interests, and ignorance regarding international affairs. The perceptions of *kairos* as glimpses of the Kingdom of God were real, but they have been buried under church bureaucratization and national security panics. The South African *Kairos Document* has approached the closest to fulfillment. Tillich saw his vision in the twentieth century as relevant to small groups, but it has grown to where it calls forth church response, and sometimes these come close to realization. When our movements fail or nearly fail, those still nurturing aspects of Tillich's thought are saved from cynicism by the same Spirit that prompted them in the first place. *Kairos* or the Kingdom of God certainly negates the outrageous wealth and desperate poverty of the present reality. Tillich knew that hope was one of the constituents of humanity.

Chapter 10

TILLICH, NIEBUHR, AND BENNETT ON THE BOMB[1]

Church leaders and the public knew nothing about the development of the atomic bomb, as decisions were made by scientists, military people, and a few civilian officials, particularly Presidents Roosevelt and Truman. On some other war-related issues, church leaders were ahead of the political leadership. Reinhold Niebuhr, for example, had told of the murder of Jews in camps as early as 1933. Paul Tillich had denounced the anti-Semitism of Nazism before it was understood in the United States. John Foster Dulles, as chairman of the Federal Council of Churches Commission, had met with President Roosevelt advocating an international organization. In 1944-45, the church was developing American opinion to reverse its shortsighted rejection of the League of Nations and to support a new and strengthened United Nations. Church leaders had denounced obliteration bombing of cities and questioned demands for unconditional

[1] Published in Mary Ann Stenger and Ronald H. Stone, *Dialogues of Paul Tillich* (Macon: Mercer University Press, 2002): 241-53.

surrender. But on the development of nuclear weapons they were silent in their innocence. On the coming of the new nuclear age, they did not see the signs of the times. Paul Tillich's brilliant *The World Situation*, published in 1945, for example, has no mention of the new warfare soon to be revealed. Meanwhile, the Manhattan project was going ahead across the street from Union Theological Seminary. The President of Union Seminary and the Editorial Board of *Christianity and Crisis* had, in June of 1945, spoken out against the single-minded slogan of unconditional surrender and against obliteration bombing. Henry Pitney van Dusen directed these two criticisms at the administration in the issue of *Christianity and Crisis* dated August 6, 1945, the day of the first atomic bombing.

The Rev. George Kennedy Bell, Bishop of Chichester, wrote:

> There are certain deeds which science should not do. There are certain actions for which scientists should not be made conscripts by any nation. And surely the extermination of any civilian population by any nation is one of these.[2]

By October of 1945, Reinhold Niebuhr saw that neither world control of atomic energy nor the outlawing of the bomb was going to be realized. He had some hope for sharing atomic knowledge in a thoroughgoing settlement of issues with the Soviet Union, but he knew that, too, was beyond immediate political realization.[3]

The earliest semi-official church statement on atomic warfare was the release in the spring of 1946 of the report of the Commission on the Relation of the Church to the War in the Light of the Christian Faith. The report is widely referred to by the name of its chairman, Robert L. Calhoun, Professor of Historical Theology, Yale University, as the "Calhoun Report." Its membership included nearly two dozen leading professors of theology and Christian

---

[2] George Kennedy Bell, "Bishop Bell Condemns Use of Atomic Bomb," *Christianity and Crisis* 5, no. 15 (September 17, 1945), 7.

[3] Reinhold Niebuhr, "The Atomic Issue," *Christianity and Crisis* 5, no. 17, (October 15, 1945), 7.

ethics, mostly from the eastern corridor of schools, including one woman and one African-American. John C. Bennett served as secretary and drafted most of the report. Throughout his long career he would continue to write, teach, and debate on these subjects. Both of the Niebuhr brothers were present.

The theology of the report is theocentric with God understood as creator, redeemer, and judge. The report, after a theological analytic preface, begins with repentance. "We would begin with an act of contrition. As American Christians we are deeply penitent for the irresponsible use already made of the atomic war." [4]

The "surprise bombings" without warning were specifically regarded as "morally indefensible." Further argument referred to the discussion among scientists of an alternative demonstrative use. Japan's position in 1945 had been hopeless, but the report conceded the bombing may have shortened the war.

The report put the atomic bomb in the context of the preatomic obliteration bombing and rejected the arguments of military necessity alone deciding the issues. They pointed to US Air Force studies which were showing that obliteration bombing had not been, on the whole, a military success. Four theses were put forward: these new methods are intolerable to Christian conscience and Christians need to resist their use, war itself is the problem, the US was urged to stop production of atomic bombs and to promise no first use, and fourthly, UN control of atomic weapons was needed.

The church's role was in helping the spirit of worldwide community to grow. Penitence for wartime crimes was called for. The temptations to over punish the vanquished enemies needed to be overcome. Hiroshima and Nagasaki should be rebuilt, and the churches could lead the financial drive. The report concluded with the final third of the report being theological analysis of ultimate

[4] Commission on the Relation of the Church to the War in the Light of the Christian Faith, "Atomic Warfare and the Christian Faith," (New York: Federal Council of Churches, 1946), 11.

issues of faith.

Robert C. Batchelder has called attention to the conditioning of the report by World War II with the expectation that war would be total war. Therefore, the war problem itself was attacked. The report focused on the tilting of the advantage to aggressive rather than defensive war and the advantage to the attacker of surprise attack or treachery.

By 1950, most of the church leaders who had condemned the bombing were learning to accept the weapons themselves and deterrence.[5] It awaited further work by ethicists and historians to refute the arguments that the bomb itself stopped the war and led to Japan's surrender or that the bomb was necessary to prevent a costly United States' invasion of Japan.

Paul Tillich shared the dilemma of the church statements following the bomb that rejected total war but did not completely renounce the bomb. The Federal Council report of the Dunn Commission of 1950 saw the need for deterrence, and they would not give up even the first possible use of the bomb. Batchelder reports that the Catholic moralists who wrote *The Ethics of Atomic War* in 1947 saw the dilemma and affirmed both the immorality of bombing a city and the possible necessity for so doing. Similarly, the British Council of Churches' *The Era of Atomic Power* could neither sanction the use of atomic weapons nor demand their abandonment in the present situation.[6] Batchelder believes the Federal Council of Churches' Commission of 1950, of which Bennett, Niebuhr, and Tillich were members, escaped the dilemma by drawing the line between bombing of cities and other uses of nuclear weapons. The moral distinctions are not between instruments in warfare. Atomic

---

[5] Robert C. Calhoun and Georgia Harkness of the original critics dissented from the Dunn Commission of 1950, which represented the theologians' acceptance of the weapons. See Robert C. Batchelder, *The Irreversible Decision 1939-1950* (Boston: Houghton Mifflin Co., 1961), 237-69.

[6] Batchelder, 250.

bombs may, under some circumstances, be used, but their indiscriminate use had to be avoided. Niebuhr's introduction to the statement in *Christianity and Crisis* calls attention to four aspects of the report.[7]

> (1) The report is set in context of historical responsibilities to defend Western civilization.
>
> (2) No absolute distinction among kinds of weapons is made morally. So the report refuses to denounce specifically all possible first uses of atomic weapons.
>
> (3) The primary task is to avoid war through development of non-Communist worlds, unity of allied nations, and international courage. Preventive war and/or inevitable war understandings are rejected.
>
> (4) The difference between destruction of military targets and mass destruction of civilian population was central to the report.

Two pacifists on the Dunn Commission who refused to sign the final report published their dissent. The context of the Dunn report was the beginning of the Korean War, and though this expressed itself in the sentences affirming the struggle with Communism, it failed to note that the present wars were limited and the nuclear weapons, while relevant, were unlikely to be used. Batchelder is very critical of these church studies in their failure to focus on limited wars. The pacifists felt that not enough distinctive Christian guidance was given and that a more thorough theological document was needed. The 1950 document was more aware of the Cold War and the Korean War and less critical of atomic weapons in themselves than the 1946 piece. The church was learning to live with the weapons.

Paul Tillich joined his Union colleagues Reinhold Niebuhr and John Bennett in signing the report. Niebuhr had endorsed the "no

[7] Reinhold Niebuhr, "Christian Conscience and Atomic War," *Christianity and Crisis* 10, no. 21, (December 11, 1950), 161.

first use of hydrogen weapons" in 1950 while conceding that in the Cold War context the United States could not refrain from developing them after the Soviet Union had detonated the atomic bomb. Seeing the Baruch plan defeated and finding little hope in nuclear disarmament negotiations with the USSR, he pleaded for restraint in US planning to rely on the bomb.[8] The arguments of no first use were the strongest recommendations of the Dunn Commission.

In Tillich's own writing he argued that a war fought with nuclear weapons could not be justified. It was not permissible to enter a war which included the intention to use nuclear weapons. Such a war would only bring mutual destruction and no intended goal of the war could be fulfilled. He noted that Western allies could, if they had the will, develop conventional armaments adequate to deter any Communist invasion in Europe. He leaned toward a position of no first use of nuclear weapons as the Commission had declared, but he also allowed the West some ambiguity in announcing such a policy. Until adequate conventional forces were created, "maybe it was safer to keep the Communists uncertain about first use."[9] However, the logic of deterrence meant: "Our intention to answer any nuclear attack with nuclear weapons must be absolutely clear, and it must also be clear that we have the power to do so."[10]

A remarkable short statement by Tillich was published in 1954 in *Pulpit Digest* on the hydrogen bomb. It consisted of only five points. Humanity may destroy itself by the tensions in itself. The meaning of history is not dependent on how humanity is annihilated. Resistance to self-destruction is called forth by all persons who are aware of humanity's suicidal instincts. The resistance must be carried out in all levels of politics, morals, and religions including "a

[8] Reinhold Niebuhr, "The Hydrogen Bomb," *Christianity and Society* (Spring 1950), 5-7.

[9] Paul Tillich, "Correspondence," *Partisan Review* 39, no. 2 (1962): 311-12.

[10] Tillich, 312.

new expression of the ultimate concern which transcends as well as determines historical existence."[11] Finally, the acts of resistance must unite all these different levels of concern and be done with wisdom and courage. The emphasis on resistance to human self-destruction was new, and it did not simply follow Niebuhr and Bennett.

The correspondence in the Harvard Archive indicates that Tillich was repeatedly requested by the American Friends Service Commission, the National Committee for a Sane Nuclear Policy, and other organizations to endorse their positions against weapons testing and for nuclear disarmament. He refused to give any of the organizations wholehearted support, and he especially resisted their pacifist leanings. He did sign a statement of the Committee for a Sane Nuclear Policy in 1957 calling for arms control and the abolition of nuclear testing. The statement was published in *The New York Times* on November 15, 1957. Other signatures included long standing pacifists, anti-war activists, religious leaders, Eleanor Roosevelt, and John Bennett, whose guidance Tillich often sought on these questions. Reinhold Niebuhr, who was a little more of a Cold Warrior than John Bennett, refrained from signing, though on most issues Bennett, Niebuhr, and Tillich were agreed. Tillich's Harvard secretary, Grace Leonard, was a member of SANE, and through her influence, Tillich agreed to SANE's 1961 use of his statement in the *Pulpit Digest* on resistance to the hydrogen bomb.

After Reinhold Niebuhr's stroke in 1952, John Bennett, the younger colleague of both Niebuhr and Tillich, took the lead in writing the frequent articles and essays in *Christianity and Crisis*. Though mindful of the full context of the Cold War, Bennett would focus his direct attention on the problems of the weapons themselves. Niebuhr always accentuated not the weapons but the conflict which gave rise to the weapons. Tillich made shorter contributions

[11] Reprinted in Paul Tillich, "The Hydrogen Bomb," in *Theology of Peace* (Louisville: Westminster/John Knox Press, 1990), 158-59.

to the discussion which revealed great passion and deep concern about the problem, but he was not the leader. Bennett's recollection, shortly before his death in 1995, was that Niebuhr's thought provided the leadership on this issue. But it was Bennett who edited the book *Nuclear Weapons and the Conflict of Conscience*; Niebuhr wrote a very laudatory review of it.

Niebuhr's major contribution was the chapter "The Cold War and the Nuclear Dilemma" in his 1959 volume, *The Structure of Nations and Empires*.[12] He could find no way out of the dilemma which was the necessity of possessing the weapons and the moral impossibility of using them. All three of the Christian realists recognized the need, in a nuclear age, for the deterrence, but all of them were horrified at thoughts of first use, preventive war, or preventive strike use of the weapons. Accepting that neither side intended to initiate a major conflict, it could still come upon them. Even so, the prospects for either disarmament or arms control seemed minor until the hostilities of the Cold War faded. Capitulation of the allied side seemed unrealistic to Niebuhr, though some in the West advocated it. He did not expect capitulation from the Communist side except in the long range of hundreds of years. Attempts to limit the conflict to tactical weapons in Europe, as Kissinger had proposed, did not seem realistic to Niebuhr in 1959, though he had hailed Kissinger's book when it first came out. His one hope was in the waning of the communist fervor as the original generations of revolutionary idealists faded from the scene. We were not fated to confront fanatical communism forever, but communism was perceived to have advantages in the third world, and he did not see its demise in the foreseeable future. Occasionally, reports of scientific dialogue between scientists from the USA and the USSR, the ABM treaty, or the partial test ban treaty would raise his hopes that incremental

---

[12] Reinhold Niebuhr, "The Cold War and the Nuclear Dilemma," in *The Structure of Nations and Empires* (New York: Charles Scribner's Sons, 1959), 267-86.

steps might add up to significant progress in relationships with the USSR, but his overall perspective was pessimistic, and he expected ongoing conflict mediated by fears of mutual annihilation and processes of wise diplomacy.

BERLIN

The dangers of the 1961 Berlin crisis led to Paul Tillich's participation in the debates again. It is hard for us to remember the sense of danger that accompanied the Kennedy years of presidency. I was in Europe during the summer of 1961, and I particularly remember the sense of crisis and the foreboding dark fears of pessimism of Norman Vincent Peale, with whom I was visiting in Interlaken. Informed people knew that Berlin was near the crux of the Cold War and that the young president was being tested very threateningly by Khrushchev. Tillich, with the realism of his own theology and his central European experience, could not regard shifts in the borders of Berlin or its politics as the ultimate issue. His appearance on a panel discussion of Eleanor Roosevelt's with Henry Kissinger, James Reston, and Max Freedman revealed the deep caution with which Tillich regarded the use of nuclear weapons. The panel was dominated by the hard line Cold Warriors. A few days later James Reston attacked Tillich for Tillich's refusal to defend Berlin with nuclear weapons.[13] For Tillich defense was a moral necessity, but to defend something in actions which meant its destruction violated the reason for defense. Particularly noteworthy in Tillich's analysis, a theme that appeared elsewhere in his writing during this period, is the insight that even retreat is not the end. Retreat is a normal strategic move. He knew and wrote in *Partisan Review* in 1962 that in the long run the West was militarily superior to the Warsaw Pact nations. The avoidance of retreat was no excuse for relying on nuclear weapons in a

[13] James Keston, "Kennedy in the Middle on German Debate," *The New York Times*, October 25, 1961.

suicidal manner.

The Christian realists quickly picked up the debate in November 1961.[14] Bennett led by calling for more significant participation in these nuclear moral issues and cautioning about any violation of the firebreak between conventional and nuclear weapons use. Niebuhr added a short response agreeing that the only use of the weapons for the West was in deterrence or in a second strike to prevent any further attacks by the enemy who had already unleashed nuclear weapons. Kenneth Thompson, in the same issue, refused to go to the no first use position and cautioned Bennett against strident moral protest. Tillich published the statement which had led to the attacks on his recommendation of no nuclear defense of his home city of Berlin with nuclear weapons. Tillich's statement was a shortened form of his own formulation of the justified war position. Proportionality was built into the requirement that any recourse to war must serve creative justice. Atomic war, he concluded, cannot be justified ethically. Therefore, while defense was required, temporary retreat until the allies could restore the conventional forces was an ordinary tactic and was preferred to any imitation of a nuclear exchange. The criticisms directed at this no first use policy of these Christian realists was that it invited attack to telegraph beforehand that you would not defend a vulnerable position with nuclear weapons. For their part the Christian realists regarded the first use of atomic weapons as wrong, and they did not want to be the first to use them ever again.

SUMMARY

Christian realism, as I understand it from my reading of these two thinkers and the additional contributions of Bennett, had several distinctive emphases. The atomic bombing of Hiroshima and Nagasaki was morally wrong. Cities should never be the object of

---

[14] *Christianity and Crisis* 21, no. 19 (November 13, 1961) 200-204.

nuclear weapon attack or obliteration bombing in warfare. It was necessary to retain nuclear weapons as long as one's enemy possessed them. It was morally wrong to use nuclear weapons first. The danger of war remained even though neither superpower intended to begin a nuclear exchange. Incremental reduction of the danger of war and the decrease of nuclear terror were possible through creative diplomacy and the probing of the other's position to find out where agreement was possible. They did not foresee any near end to the Cold War, and they did not trust much in disarmament negotiations while the political issues were divisive.

After the assassination of President Kennedy, Tillich's public political role decreased, though he did, as a systematic theologian, issue a denunciation of Goldwater partially because of Goldwater's saber-rattling stances. Niebuhr followed the debates until his death in 1971, growing increasingly concerned about the dominance of the military under Presidents Johnson and Nixon in the context of the Vietnam War. Bennett's debates with Paul Ramsey continued the Christian realist debates. Bennett exalted over the collapse of the USSR and the decrease in the nuclear dangers. In his last Christmas letter he quoted Simeon, "Now let thy servant depart in peace."

In conclusion, I find a lot of wisdom in this review of Christian realism. During his lifetime, I disagreed with Reinie on the evil of Communism. Now, I think he was more correct than I was. Bennett was not in agreement with my criticism of deterrence as immoral. Its intention to be used under certain circumstances against enemy civilians rendered it morally indefensible, as I argued in *The Peacemaking Struggle*, 1985, and *Presbyterians and Peacemaking: Are We Now Called to Resistance*, 1985 (both with Dana Wilbanks), and

Christian Realism and Peace Making, 1988.[15] I do not think Reinhold Niebuhr or Paul Tillich would have put it the way I did either. Niebuhr left it at the dilemma level, with the only possible use in defensive strike. Tillich stayed with the use of war only as an act of creative justice and did not reject deterrence. I thought and think that the Christian moralist must reject nuclear deterrence morally and then urge creative solutions moving us away from reliance on nuclear weapons. I do not think the moral rejection of deterrence means policies of surrender or immediate unilateral disarmament. That is not how policy works. The Christian moralist fulfills the vocation by saying as clearly as possible what is intolerable and working with others to find ways to move out of the morally impossible structures.

Niebuhr warned us as well as anyone about the imponderables, surprises, and ironies of history. I will not criticize him, now, for not foreseeing the early end of the Soviet Empire. My own reading is that the collapse was mostly due to the failure of the ideas of communism and this is quite ironic for a historical materialist system. Maybe he was a little too pessimistic about arms control agreements, but not very much. His optimism was probably more misplaced in his hopes for UNESCO and the Alliance for Progress. At this point it seems useful to me to note that this Christian Realism was quite different from government policy, though McNamara's strategies brought the government closer to the realist sense of morality. Though it often found wisdom in Kissinger, Kahn, and other mainstream nuclear theorists, the moral reservations and critique were present. Notes of unilateral initiatives recommended by Bennett and

---

[15] Ronald H. Stone, "The Justifiable War Tradition," in Ronald H. Stone and Dana Wilbanks, eds., *The Peacemaking Struggle: Militarism and Resistance* (Lanham: University Press of America, 1985), 185-95; Dana Wilbanks and Ronald H. Stone, *Presbyterians and Peacemaking: Are We Now Called to Resistance* (New York: Advisory Council on Church and Society, 1985), 10-24; Ronald H. Stone, *Christian Realism and Peace Making* (Nashville: Abingdon Press, 1988), 86-101.

Tillich's resistance to nuclear weapons and the necessity of relying on conventional defense took these Christian realists a long way from harder realism or realpolitik and US government policy. Finally, Tillich's refusal to regard even atomic warfare as ultimate kept it in perspective. Ultimately, there was God and not decisions by politicians or generals.

Chapter 11

ETHICS AND THE ENCOUNTER WITH OTHER RELIGIONS

Tillich was cognizant of the questions other religions raised since he had written his dissertation on Friedrich Schelling for the University of Breslau, "The Conception of the History of Religions in Schelling's Positive Philosophy: Its Presuppositions and Conclusions" in 1910. His work had always, since World War I, been in conversation with Jewish philosophers and social scientists, and his writings on Judaism were considered in chapter three. Late in life his thought and conversation expanded to studies on Buddhism. Particularly before his death in 1965, he engaged with Buddhists, lectured on the encounter of Christianity with other religions, and completed the seminar on world religions at the University of Chicago with Mircea Eliade. I heard his lectures at Columbia University in 1961 after his trip to encounter Zen Buddhism in Japan. By this time, as a beginning Master of Divinity student at Union Theological Seminar, I had read volume 1 of the *Systematic Theology* and worked a little on his theory of symbol. I was a novice in Tillich studies. The next summer I would explore symbol in Tillich's thought further in studies with Langdon Gilkey, who had just returned from linguistic studies at Oxford University. But these particulars are not the reason for including reflection on *Christianity and the Encounter of the World Religions* in a book on his ethics. His quest for peace requires cooperation and understanding dialogue among the world religions. It would never have occurred to Tillich that serious peace studies could be undertaken without work on the relationships among religions. But the content of the book itself is more about the subject matter of religious social ethics than it is about the metaphysical relations and agreements or disagreements between Buddhism and Christianity.

The dialogues of Paul Tillich are very personal. The presentations of the Zen Masters similarly reflect their personal perspectives as much as Tillich's perspective is his own. No student of theology or religion would mistake Tillich's form of Christianity for that of Karl Barth or that of Reinhold Niebuhr. His version of Christianity is his own. My chapter is also personal, drawing upon my career long relationship with Jewish scholars of religion at Columbia University and the University of Pittsburgh. A Jew first told me not to consider going to Claremont School of Theology, because he wanted to hire me for Columbia. I presented at various locations of Jewish-Christian dialogue in Pittsburgh as well as at the University. In India, my dialogues were naturally and regularly with Hindus. Despite minor occasional dialogues previously, my work on Islam only became serious after 9/11, and it took me to conversations in Lebanon, Syria, Jordan, Egypt, and Israel. Christian Orthodox conversations occurred in Belgrade, Athens, Istanbul, Prague, and Moscow. But unfortunately my serious conversations with Buddhist monks only occurred in Bhutan in 2013, so I am still a novice in that exploration, despite teaching Buddhism in 1969 at Columbia University. My daughter's marriage to a former Buddhist Priest promises further dialogues when he reads the chapter.

Professor Thomas Tangaraj arranged a trip and a talk with

Professor Gangadaran at the Meenakshi-Siva Temple in Madurai. It was the first major temple for the children, Randy, Jessica, John, and Patricia. The ten tall gopurams (towers) are decorated with hundreds of Hindu deities in polychrome colors. The room of a thousand pillars has pillars decorated with more Hindu gods and scenes from the life of India in the seventeenth century. Professor Gangadaran furnished a short introduction to the children on Hindu mythology. We, at his direction, wandered through the temple. I was surprised when he prostrated himself before the idol of Nanda, the bull. He explained to me that he assumed the peasants prayed to the bull, but his puja was an act to the one God, Brahmin. Then, as we watched the bathers in the pool, he explained to me the difference between symbols and signs and how the symbols participated in the power of the living deity. We then drifted into a discussion of Paul Tillich, and he asserted that most of the Hindu philosophers who participated in Christian-Hindu dialogue, like himself and the Christian Seminary Professor Tangaraj, were Tillichians to some degree. Years later, while he was a visiting professor at Harvard, I met him and took him on a tour of Concord and Lexington where so many of my ancestors had fought the British. The two encounters provided a clue to some of the dialogues between Eastern and Christian religion; many of the participants are already well versed not only in Western philosophy but also in the thought of Tillich before the dialogue begins. This is a preliminary point for the interpretation of the dialogues of Tillich with the Buddhists of Japan, with whom he so significantly dialogues.

PRE-JAPAN DIALOGUES WITH BUDDHISM

In 1957, Dr. Hisamatsu Shin'ichi and Paul Tillich met three times at Harvard Divinity School for conversations about Zen Buddhism and Tillich's theology. Tillich began the conversation asking how Zen could help him meditate and develop the vertical dimension of his life in the midst of his busy schedule of lectures around the country. Hisamatsu advised him to set aside a special period in his daily schedule, but also, as in the heart of Zen, to find a place of calmness amidst his business.

Hisamatsu continued by explaining "calm self" to Tillich. He meant to be speaking about the "No-Mind" or "No Consciousness." Hisamatsu tried to explain with a metaphor of eyes "seeing" and also by reference to Meister Eckhart's negation. Further discussion led to Zen finding the Formless Self while Tillich's Christianity finds the *logos* and *agape*. The two philosophers agreed Tillich remained dualistic while Zen overcame it. They could agree on preference for expressionism in art. However Tillich needed distinctions between subject and object which disappeared in the Formless Self.1

Hisamatsu found *Guernica* too noisy and not a work of the Formless Self. They agreed art in both East and West was expressing secularism. They concluded with Hisamatsu wanting to learn more about "God beyond God" and "Courage to be," while Tillich needed to learn more about the practice of Zen.

The second dialogue with Hisamatsu continued the discussion of Zen art. Mrs. Tillich had been attending his lectures and was inspired by his handling the relationship of art to the Ultimate. The translators entered the discussion more deeply than in the first dialogue. One of them, De Martino, summarized the major point of difference between the two as for Tillich "the depth of being" led to God as the source, whereas for Hisamatsu it led to the true or Formless Self.[2] Tillich throughout the conversation could never accept the combination of universality, non-being, and non-self affirmed by the Buddhists.

Hisamatsu asked about the foundations of religion, as that was his seminar subject at Harvard. Tillich answered preliminarily that

---

[1] Paul Tillich and Hisamatsu Shin'ichi, "Dialogues: East and West, Part One," *The Eastern Buddhist* 4, no. 2 (October 1971), 93.

[2] Paul Tillich and Hisamatsu Shin'ichi, "Dialogues: East and West, Part Two," *The Eastern Buddhist* 5, no. 2 (October 1972), 110.

the human was related to the infinite and excluded from it. He said he used the word "infinite' and not the word "God" in De Martino's summary. Tillich summarized his thought as: (1) The infinite is the creative ground of the finite, (2) the infinite is the judge of the finite, and (3) the infinite is the reunion with the finite. Further reunion is the aim of religion.[3]

Tillich's ethics were summarized as the good overcoming evil or the human acting against evil. Tillich opted for anticipating fulfillment of the good in history and the total fulfillment in the infinite, which reduced evil to potentiality. Hisamatsu, without the infinite, argued for the total fulfillment of the Formless Self. As Tillich pushed Hisamatsu, the Formless Self receded in his argument beyond time and space. Neither thinker could reconcile to accept the other's position. Hisamatsu wanted to escape the dualism he detected in Tillich, who regarded the gap between humanity and the infinite and good and evil as unbridgeable. For Hisamatsu, Buddhist awakening produced a new person. Tillich also recognized New Being in Paul's thought, but in history, as Paul recognized, the struggle still continued. But for Hisamatsu, the Awakening overcame time and space. I sympathize with Hisamatsu's, "Yes; but with the Awakening, being just an 'ordinary human' comes to an end."[4] But I also know the time and space that comes with conversion and the continued failure to find unity with the perfection of the infinite or in one's own life.

In the third dialogue, the interpreter, Richard De Martino, assumed the major role, while Hisamatsu remained the distant authority on Zen. His book, translated later into English as *Zen and the Fine Arts*, was in the background in the discussion of Zen art.

The discussion focused on the relationship of the particular and the ultimate. Tillich insisted on the particularity of an object, though

[3] Tillich and Hisamatsu, "Dialogues, Part Two," 112.

[4] Tillich and Hisamatsu, "Dialogues, Part 2," 124.

it participated in the Ultimate. For the Zen participants, the particular was the ultimate and not the ultimate. Tillich refused to say he was the ultimate, while it was not a problem for the Zen Buddhists.

This conversation and the different expressions of individuality and universality would continue in Tillich's later conversations in Japan and lead him to doubt whether the individual was regarded enough in particularity to support the democracy inherited in Japan from the Americans.

As they focused on selected works of art, Tillich, in his love for the yellow flower under discussion, could go so far as to say he was a nature mystic. De Martino reminded him he was a German nature mystic. Tillich would deny neither the particularity nor the universal, both of which were of less interest to the Buddhist in their disappearance in the Formless Self.[5]

In Japan, the dialogue with Hisamatsu was renewed in his rock garden in the summer of 1960. The same theme of universality or a particularity with participation of the garden in the universe continued.6 Tillich summarized his findings in his report on Japan:

> The discussions with Buddhists have shown to me that the main points of difference are always: the different valuation of the individual person, of religious and social reformation, of the meaning of history, of the interpersonal relations of finitude and guilt. It is the contrast between the principle of identity and the principle of participation. It seems to me that, although the principles are exclusive, the actual life of both Christianity, especially in its Protestant from, and Buddhism, especially in its monastic form, could receive elements from each other without losing their basic character.[7]

---

[5] Paul Tillich and Hisamatsu Shin'ichi, "Dialogues: East and West, Part Three," *The Eastern Buddhist* 6, no. 2 (October 2, 1973): 87-114.

[6] Paul Tillich, "Informal Report on Lecture Trip to Japan" (unpublished, Summer 1969). Copy in author's possession.

[7] Tillich, 8.

The Tillichs' trip was carefully arranged for them by The Committee for Intellectual Exchange. For nine weeks, they appreciated the complete graciousness of their Japanese hosts, with six weeks in Tokyo and three weeks in Kyoto with brief trips to other shrines. He met with old friends, preached twice, and toured with carefully selected guides and priests to many of the important Buddhist, Shinto, and New Religions' shrines. He remarked often on the ancient traditions, religions, and art they experienced. But the new secularism was pressing in upon the Japanese, young people trying to escape the past.

Political tensions were discussed, as President Eisenhower planned a visit to arrange for the rearming of Japan. They found very little anti-Americanism, though they heard of it in the Communist parties and activists. Tillich dismissed the relevance of Communism to Japan. He was very busy lecturing and participating in organized discussions mostly on theology and culture.

Following his conversation with Hisamatsu, Tillich had a similar conversation with twenty scholars and fifty students at Otani University in Kyoto. He reported to the Christian Center for the Study of Japanese Religions near Kyoto. They had asked him to speak about the demonic. He explained that he thought the demonic encouraged idolatry and suppressed justice. The Christians asked him about his conclusions from the discussions with Buddhists. He insisted that discussions did not have conclusions. He expressed that he had chosen to ask three questions of the Buddhists: (1) What is the difference between popular Buddhist piety and the scholar's metaphysics? (2) How do the scholars deal with demonic in mass religion? (3) Does Buddhism have something similar to the Reformation in Europe? He thought the Buddhists negated his questions. In fact, the transcript of the dialogue shows they also lacked interest in his other question about the historical truth regarding Gautama. He taught at Harvard for the fall term of 1960, and then in 1961 he brought his learnings to Columbia.

CHRISTIANITY'S ENCOUNTER WITH OTHER RELIGIONS

Lecture one by Tillich in 1961, entitled "A View of the Present Situation: Religions, Quasi-Religions, and their Encounters," surveyed the social ethics and religious themes of movements of the late twentieth century that had impacted Tillich and his times. Tillich regarded himself as an observer participant in the encounters with other faiths. That is, he participated as a Christian, but he tried to be as objective as possible in his reporting.

Tillich's definition of religion was the state of being grasped by ultimate concern of a tradition that provides a perspective on the meaning of life.8 It is inclusive enough to include Fascism, Communism, Nationalism, and Secularism as religions, or, as he prefers, quasi-religions. The main engagement of the world religions is with the quasi-religions, and it is in the context of technological advancement encouraging secularism or an indifference to traditional religion. Fascism, Nationalism, and Communism all attack religion within the context of twentieth century secularism which had already weakened religion. Tillich was not sanguine about the ability of liberal humanism's democracy being able to survive. Historical development has moved beyond Tillich's types, with Communism being replaced in Russia by a nationalistic dictatorship professing loyalty to Russian-Christian Orthodoxy, and in China a nationalistic capitalism has replaced Communism, though some of its mythical structure remains. India has chosen a militant Hinduism which Tillich did not anticipate, and Islam has arisen in Jihadist-Islamic expressions. Technology has shaken off its liberal, humanistic origins and developed tendencies towards authoritarianism. The religious indifference spawned from secularism continues, particularly

[8] Paul Tillich, *Christianity and the Encounter of World Religions* (New York: Columbia University Press, 1963), 4. Paul Tillich, *Christianity and the Encounter of World Religions* (New York: Columbia University Press, 1963), 4.

in the west, but also in Japan. He suggested the encounters of traditional world religions with these quasi-religious movements were the most important part of the encounters. In the subsequent sixty years, the players have changed, and in the Middle East and India religious-political movements have dominated the more secular Western influences. Tillich neglected to study Islam in depth, and its developments have eclipsed his judgments that Islam would dominate Sub-Saharan Africa. The surprising power of conservative religion to overwhelm traditional elite-secular forces as, for example, in the Republican Party in the USA could not be foreseen in the early 1960s. Religious politics have in many scenes become more, not less, important than Tillich recorded in the 1960s.

In lecture two Tillich adopts a sharper Christian perspective on the encounter with other religions as he recognizes it belongs to the Christian participant to confess his role that Jesus is the Christ and to reject views that deny such a conclusion. The rejection is a dialectical one which can be joined with appreciation of various aspects of other religions. It is a yes/no approach which often characterizes his thinking. He finds this dialectical acceptance and rejection of other traditions to be characteristic of Christianity.

Even in Christianity in its origins in the Old Testament other religious traditions are accepted in part and rejected in part. He reads Amos not so much as the rejecting prophet as he does as one who finds universal religion in the universality of justice and bases his monotheism on the reality of the universality of justice. Tillich finds Jesus not being so particular about his tradition's law but finding value in the Good Samaritan, all nations which have acted righteously in Matthew 25, the universal concept of logos, and with the Samaritan woman. According to Tillich, Paul regards Jews and pagans as standing equally in judgment before God, and aspects of Stoic ethics and Greek mystery religions can be found in Paul. The early church fathers continued the universal thrust in that whatever was true belonged to Christianity. Christianity could accept Greek concepts from its Hellenistic context, the legal tradition from Rome, and even Germanic customs and hierarchic realities as it expanded into Northern Europe. It was easier for Christianity to be tolerant of, and even the borrower from, other traditions as long as it had no need to recognize another as competitor. Tillich sees the competition with Islam as driving Christianity toward exclusivism and eventually into the Crusades against Islam. Attitudes toward Judaism hardened at the same time and prepared the ground first for anti-Judaism and later anti-Semitism.

The longest part of the lecture described Christian universalism from Cardinal Nicholas Cusanus to the Berlin theologian/historian Ernst Troeltsch. Troeltsch could find in Christ an absolute for European civilization but not for rest of the world. The missionary drive should be altered toward "cross fertilization" of religions. Philosophers of religion, while sometimes regarding Christianity as the highest form of religion, also laid the groundwork for relativism regarding religions. Tillich admitted the majority of theologians were probably absolutists and exclusivists regarding Christianity, but obviously he counted himself among the Universalists while retaining the self-surrendering of Jesus as absolute. He understood the best of Protestantism as open to some secular themes and particularly open or vulnerable to the liberal humanist developments. He feared particularly the temptation of some conservative Protestants to merge their religion with the nationalist apostasy.[9]

His third lecture was on his own dialogue with Buddhism, but as the lecture was given on a basic level for those who might not know much about Buddhism, he kept it simple. Depth can be achieved only with some of the records of his own dialogues. Following Max Weber, I believe, he placed his discussion on types drawn from religious experience. The religious life is never only in types of experience in purity, because in real life one individual or

[9] Tillich, *Encounter*, 50.

religion is a mixture of types. He thought religion could be illustrated by the use of polar types, such as mysticism or ethics. Indian religions were more mystical, and the Abrahamic religions were more of the ethical type.

He stated that Buddhism and Christianity had not encountered each other in basic ways as religions. At this point in 1961, or at least by the time the book was published in 1963, he should have noted Christian oppression of Buddhists in Indochina. French Catholicism had been defeated by Buddhists under Communist-Indochinese leadership as early as 1954, and the Roman Church in America was cooperating with secular leaders to defend Catholic Mandarins' power in South Vietnam. He recognized that his fellow Union Theological Board Member had imposed peace upon the Japanese.[10] John Foster Dulles had concluded the peace agreement for Truman, disarming Japan and guaranteeing the USA military bases. The more militant Buddhists of Vietnam needed recognition while perhaps using poles of pacifism and militarism to describe Buddhist-Christian poles for the dialogue. By the time the book was published, students at Union Theological Seminary were protesting US involvement in Vietnam and naming themselves after Madame Nhu's words of contempt for Buddhist monks, *Les Petit Predicateurs.*

Tillich did have one reference to the development of more militancy in some of Buddhism, but the years of conquests of Christians over Buddhists in Malaysia, Thailand, Burma, Ceylon, China, and Japan were mostly ignored. The notation that the symbols of Kingdom of God and Nirvana represented poles within the religions could have explored not only terms of individuation and participation but terms of political activism and relative inaction in history, as seen in the conquest of Buddhist lands by Christians.

Tillich's criteria for dialogue were: (1) Both partners

[10] Louis L. Gerson, *John Foster Dulles* (New York: Cooper Square Publishers, 1967), 29.

acknowledge the worth of both traditions; (2) Conviction of one's own tradition, so that the confrontation is serious; (3) The presupposition of a common ground; (4) The recognition of the impact of the quasi-religions upon the times and the discussion.

Mary Ann Stenger has investigated Masao Abe's writings about Tillich/Buddhist dialogue after Tillich's death, and she suggests Tillich may have overestimated the contrasts between Nirvana and the Kingdom of God. They have their differences, but Abe is passionate about expressing the regard for the society in Nirvana, and he is not so sure Christians will not be disappointed in their hurry to transform the world with their symbol of the Kingdom of God. She agrees with the later insight of Abe that "Tillich portrays Buddhism as more non-historical than it really is."[11] As Tillich noted, it is very difficult as a nonparticipant to enter exactly into the religions of the East. Tillich's point is in part an ethics question concerning the revolutionary impact of the Kingdom of God upon the Western World and not being knowledgeable about Nirvana's having a similar force. Abe agrees that the Buddhist concept could use more of an emphasis upon justice. Certainly in history Christianity could have used more of the concept of compassion and acceptance of others more associated with the Kyoto School of Zen.

The conclusion of lecture three lifted up the ethics of politics question: Given that the USA enforced democracy upon Japan, does the Shinto-Buddhist synthesis have the resources to protect it? Sometimes Tillich suggests it is the observer's question, as he does here. Other times, he suggests the question comes from his Zen interlocutor. It stems from Tillich's position that Christianity has more of an emphasis on the independence and rights of the individual. On another current question of passionate concern, Tillich

---

[11] Mary Ann Stenger, "Tillich's Idea of History as a Challenge in his Dialogues with Buddhists" in *Paul Tillich-interprete de L'histoiere*, eds. Marc Dumas, Martin Leiner, and Jean Richard (Berlin: Lit Verlag Dr. W. Hopf, 2013), 129-44.

assumes the Buddhist identity with nature emphasis makes it a better witness for protection of the earth than does the human centered view of the west founded in Genesis.

The final lecture of his small book summarizes the import of the previous lectures and speaks about the role of judgment in the interreligious dialogue. For Tillich, the only point of judgment is to be found in Jesus, who gave up his particularity in the crucifixion to express the universality of Christ as the principle of critique of religion starting with Christianity. Throughout the lecture, he argues for the importance of a religion to express its critical spirit of religious particularities. He argued that for Christianity, Christ was the only principle of judgment of Christianity and other religions. This assertion does not seem very productive for interreligious dialogue. The criteria of justice, love, or compassion can be expressed universally better than the symbol "Christ." He suggested it was "the principle of love in him embraces the cosmos."[12] In my opinion there is no need to go to "one point" for the criteria of evaluating religion if one wants the evaluation.

Tillich wisely does not want to attempt to form one common religion. He regards it as impossible to annul religion, which is founded in the nature of the human reflecting the nature of the universe and the manifestation of God. He sees no need to convert others from the major religions. Rather, it is important they find their depth in freedom. His conclusion to reflecting upon dialogue is in the finding of "spiritual freedom" for oneself and in the ultimate expressions of other religions as they reveal the meaning of human existence. For me, the discovery of the passion for justice in my dialogue partners in the Middle East has been the defining moment of interreligious dialogue. This has usually been in the search for peace. These breakthroughs were nearly three decades after listening to Tillich's lectures at Columbia. Claude Perrottet has discerned the

[12] Tillich, *Encounter*, 82.

mutual attractions of Tillich and the Zen masters.13 Friendships were formed. Hisamatsu and others were respected in the West. Their thought could not be accepted by Tillich's analytical method or his provisional tendency toward dualism. The search for the dialogue materials for help in ethics could not be fruitful. Tillich would write his own ethics books without reference to the dialogues of only a few months previously. Other than recognizing that neither the Zen masters nor Tillich were legalistic, little about ethics was mentioned. However, on the macro level, the dialogue meetings themselves were acts of reconciliation. Without much more religious dialogue and reconciliation, peace remains a utopian hope. Total peace, as Tillich knew, belongs to the Kingdom of God, but before humanity gets there much remains to be accomplished. Few others have made as much effort to dialogue at a high theological level. As Hannah recorded, he could not be accepted as Zen as he still worried about good and evil, guilt and forgiveness. Tillich's first question to Hisamatsu revealed his quest for a calmness that Hannah said he could never fulfill.[14]

---

[13] Claude Perrottet, "Guide to the Perplexed: An Attempt to Make Sense of the Tillich-Hisamatsu Dialogues" *Bulletin of the North American Paul Tillich Society* 37, no. 2 (Spring 2011): 47-62.

[14] Hannah Tillich, *From Time*, 240.

Chapter 12

LATE ETHICS: CRITIQUE AND PROJECTION

Tillich's ethics are constituted by continuity and change. The interpreter of his ethics realizes that in the *Systematic Theology* he absorbs his philosophic ethic into his theology. He stays within the Christian tradition, and it answers to science, other religions, social and psychological sciences, and to a philosophy of life.

Part four of his system is on the philosophy of life understood ontologically in its two dimensions of essence and existence. Consequently, life and the dimensions of its morals are understood to be characteristically ambiguous. The recognition of the ambiguity of morals could be regarded as a fundamental principle of his ethics.

Tillich's theology rejects supernaturalism and the hierarchical theology of the levels of being and explains life in terms of the dimensions of reality. "A new understanding of the term spirit of life is a theological necessity."[1] Spirit is taken to mean the unity of meaning and power and, consequently, includes reason.

---

[1] Tillich, *Systematic*, vol. 3, 22.

The spirit carries connotations of the earlier term *soul*, and it recognizes evolution from the nonorganic to the organic and through eons to the creature of the human spirit. The human arises from psychological and contextual forces and, in the realization of the human, fulfills the meaning of morality. Morality, to be morality, is the free acceptance of norms. Freedom here means the acting upon psychological material to affirm norms within historical and biological destiny.

The norms arise from pragmatic, or value, choices and the decisive ontological reason. Neither value theory nor pragmatism provides satisfactory answers to the relationship of their norms to being. Without deeper resources they remain arbitrary. Therefore, the need for ontology, and ultimately religion, in the sense of ultimate concern is recognized.

Life actualizes the potential of humanity's being and also realizes the potential of other beings while losing much particularity. The choices of human life for norms and of moving forward involve courage and risk taking and the sacrifice of choices not taken. "Life is neither essential nor existential, but ambiguous."[2]

Within his philosophy of the ambiguities of life, morality is the action of self-centered interpretation of one's spirit into community. This process continues throughout life. This enables the free activity of choosing norms to influence reality and to risk the application of the normative to the world.

Bryan L. Wagoner, commenting on *The Socialist Decision*, captured what could be regarded as the third characteristic of his ethics.

> What is important is not merely what humanity is, but what it can be and can do; what is crucial to Tillich, both existentially and

---

[2] Tillich, 32.

ethically is not so much essence but rather transforming possibility.[3]

The human is known not only by the environment but also by choices. The ought partially arrives from the is but also acts to transform it toward the future and, ideally, in terms of its own essential being. The human becomes responsible by choosing to serve the appropriate norm.

In the context of the dynamics of life, Tillich, in his later books, reserves the term ethics for the science of morals.[4] He surrounds his definition with two sentences freeing *moral* from its overuse in regard to sexual morals. Such odd construction reflects his own concern that his erotic choices may be a failure. However we puzzle over this worry of his, it is clear that for the later Tillich, ethics is the theory of morals. This study assumes these definitions in all of his later writing to be normative for his thought.

Mark Lewis Taylor's definition as the study of ethos is accurate for German writings as in *The System of the Sciences* and *The Socialist Decision*.5 Ethos disappears from *Systematic Theology*, and the religious study of ethics is accommodated under his very early term of "Theology of Culture." The dominant socialist commitments of the early writings obscure the examination of morals and the concept of justice in the teleological passion of overthrowing the system.

Tillich's ethics recognizes the libido wants "to win the whole world."[6] The limit to the human is in the reality of the other person. In the other person in community the moral norms limiting one's actions appear. Tillich recognizes the need to overcome some limits,

---

[3] Bryan L. Wagoner, *Prophetic Interruptions: Critical Theory, Emancipation, and Religion in Paul Tillich, Theodor Adorno, and Max Horkheimer (1929-1944)* (Macon: Mercer University Press, 2017), 207.

[4] Tillich, *Systematic*, vol. 3, 39.

[5] Bryan L. Wagoner, *Prophetic Interruptions: Critical Theory, Emancipation, and Religion in Paul Tillich, Theodor Adorno, and Max Horkheimer (1929-1944)* (Macon: Mercer University Press, 2017), 207.

[6] Tillich, *Systematic*, vol. 1, 40.

particularly irrelevant traditions or totalitarian demands. The post-revolutionary Weimar Republic threw off many norms, and Tillich led in demanding reform of church and society and in shucking off the marital norms of his parents.

The starkness of medical ethics insisting "Do no harm" points to the need for higher recognition of limits. The neglect of the limiting quality of morals frees humans to desire and express their own perceptions of self-fulfillment too easily, to the harm of immediate family and neighbors. The United States has been particularly neglectful of the norms against covetousness and greed. Social ethics, partially descended from socialism in the church, recognizes that communities which limit individuals lack the centers of moral decision to control their own actions as thoughtfully as they limit individuals.

For Tillich, life is the ambiguous struggle between choices for potential overriding other choices and the need for sacrifice of some potential for the road chosen. Many humans in poverty and ignorance have limited choices and little opportunity of realizing potentiality. All human life is in conflict and remains unfulfilled.

The moral imperative of love or recognition of the person's self is absolute, but it is a general imperative without particulars. Love as the general law is applied through justice, which takes account of the particulars. The actual rules of morality are summarized by love which understands the situation. Moral laws are valid as they express the essence of humanity over against existential estrangement.[7]

Tillich stresses the moral ambiguity of the moral norms and their expression in law. All norms reflect their historical origins and their reception in particular contexts. He moves toward moral relativism, but then he moves back toward Kant's moral formalism, recognizing the validity of love and its ultimacy. He stresses the Ten Commandments' connection to Hebrew culture, but I would stress

[7] Tillich, *Systematic*, vol. 3, 46

their continuity through approximately three thousand years and the need for contemporary interpretation. The danger is in their being abandoned, not in the necessary relatedness to origins and receptions.[8]

In the *Systematic Theology*, he argues for ethics to be determined by autonomous agreement. The theologian in work on ethics is required to be a philosopher. It is a similar position to his placement of ethics in his 1925 *The System of the Sciences.* This seems strangely abstract and bears very little relationship to the Christian child learning morals from a parent who knows a lot about the Bible but little of Hume or Kant. The nation is covered by churches in which the Ten Commandments are taught in Sunday school classes and learned by the hundreds of thousands of communicants. A theory of ethics should explicate what actually happens in the teaching of morals. Tillich's insights regarding theonomous ethics appearing in secular subjects are important, but he should not ignore what really happens in moral instruction in the country. When he writes, "theonomous morals are morals of love as a creation of the Spirit," he is fighting heteronomy, not theological ethics.[9] There is no adequate reason to assume theological ethicists are more dogmatic than philosophical ethicists. Certainly Tillich's ethics, including a God-man image, Jesus of Nazareth, and Spirit-determined, can be regarded as theological ethics even if he also uses philosophical arguments in the *Systematic Theology*.[10]

Ethics cannot escape finitude, and Tillich persistently favors love over law or norm. One could act against love either by following tradition or acting against it. Love is given as grace by the Spirit in Tillich's thought. Love is the motivating power for Christian love, *agape*. One of his best statements can be taken as his summary.

---

[8] See Stone, *The Ultimate Imperative*, 55-114.
[9] Tillich, *Systematic*, vol. 3, 272.
[10] Tillich, 274.

> Morality is determined by Spirit created love. It is supported by the Spirit created wisdom of the ages, expressed in the moral laws of the nations. It is made concrete and adequate by the application of the courage of love to the unique situation.[11]

MORALITY AND BEYOND [12]

Morality and Beyond, published the same year as the *Systematic Theology*, vol. 3, 1963, repeats in detail the arguments of his *Systematic Theology*. It places the philosophical analysis squarely in the context of theological ethics. "Theological ethics is an element of systematic theology, present in each of its parts."[13] The first three chapters were his lectures at Dartmouth College and were present in part in *Systematic Theology*. He noted some repetition and incompleteness in the book, as it was borrowed from the system. Even its dedication to Reinhold Niebuhr is interesting, as Tillich credits him for saving him from the Nazis, and he represents Niebuhr's thought as ethical while his own was ontological.

His first chapter recognizes ethics as the science of morals. The religious dimension of the moral imperative is its ultimacy or its absoluteness. It is not loyalty to any particular denomination of religion, but the insight that the religion is being grasped by ultimate concern indicates the religious dimension of morality.

Chapter two affirms the truth of relativism in that cultures reflect different norms. The relevance of natural law theory is that it shows there are common features of human morality. The point of morality is that human persons act towards their true essence of humanity. He summarized the chapter:

> To summarize the thesis of this chapter: the religious source of the moral demands is love under the domination of its *agape* quality in

---

[11] Tillich, 274.

[12] Paul Tillich, *Morality and Beyond,* ed. Ruth Nanda Anshen (New York: Harper & Row Publishers, 1963).

[13] Tillich, 13.

> unity with the imperative of justice to acknowledge every being with personal potential as a person, being guided by the divine-human wisdom embodied in the moral laws of the past, listening to the concrete situation, and acting courageously on the basis of these principles.[14]

The third chapter finds love in its many dimensions to be the maturation of moral action. He finds the law inadequate as moral motivation. As in psychotherapy he finds the motivation of true morality in the self-acceptance of acceptance as a human. The answer to motivation for this Pauline, Augustinian, Lutheran theologian is in the grace given to humanity. Mark Lewis Taylor referred to this grace as the "donative" quality of Tillich's morals.[15] The motivation is from divine love, which one accepts or rejects. It is finally *agape* not *libido*.

Paul's Romans 7 is for Tillich the most profound religious text on law in philosophy, psychology, or religion. It shows that though law can express the essence of what humanity should be, it does not motivate. God's law as understood in religion, or in Paul's case, in his Judaism, is good, but it condemns rather than motivates. In the state of estrangement, laws are compromises reflecting human law. The law in reformation thought serves the state law to deter evil action, to set a standard that drives toward repentance, and, in John Calvin, to guide the Christian that has experienced love through grace.

Tillich had argued that Christianity is particularly a religion of transforming moral action; here he expresses it as particularly a religion of grace. *Agape* includes the wisdom of moral traditions and listens to the details of particular situations. His recognition of the truth of the analysis of Paul in Romans 5-8 inclines this reader to

---

[14] Tillich, 46.

[15] Mark Lewis Taylor, "Tillich's Ethics: Between Politics and Ontology," in *The Cambridge Companion to Paul Tillich*, ed. Russell Re Manning (Cambridge: Cambridge University Press, 2009), 198-99.

wonder why he did not insert Paul's 1 Corinthians 13 to show the power of love. He concluded the three lectures:

> The unconditional character of the moral imperative, love as the ultimate source of the moral commands, and grace as the power of moral motivation are the concepts through which the relation of religion and morality is fundamentally answered.[16]

William Schweiker followed Ruth Nanda Anshen in including the two older chapters in *Morality and Beyond*.[17] The essay from 1941 is not consistent with the first three essays of the book. The chapter, "The Transmoral Conscience," is a radical chapter, but it fails to add much of importance to Tillich's ethics.[18] He recognizes the danger of transcending conscience. Did Heidegger mislead him here? Tillich implicitly accepts Heidegger's idea that humans become guilty by acting. Are we not guilty for not acting? If all acts are guilty why would we resist the Nazis? Is cooperating with such an evil government not to be resisted? Tillich confesses his debt to Heidegger and Nietzsche. They illuminated the world to him for a time. But must they be kept as sources? Rather than overriding his conscience, Tillich kept his conscience and went into exile. Bonhoeffer kept his conscience and died. Most Germans acquiesced, at least in public. Tillich called them to resist and declared them guilty when they did not resist. The idea that a sensitive conscience is sometimes a guilty conscience is sometimes true but not necessarily. Better to follow conscience and educate the conscience to new insights rather than to overcome it. My first course in philosophy was on Nietzsche, and I assisted John Macquarrie, one of Heidegger's translators, in teaching theology. But neither one of these very guilty philosophers taught me much that I cannot learn elsewhere in the tradition. Tillich himself could not move gladly beyond his

---

[16] Tillich, 64.

[17] Paul Tillich, *Morality and Beyond*, ed. William Schweiker (Louisville: Westminster/John Knox Press, 1995).

[18] Tillich, 65-81.

conscience, as his frequent references to his own guilt shows.

In the last chapter of the book written in 1941 before America awoke to the threat of Nazism, he presented the weaknesses of three systems of ethics: the Roman Catholic Church, the dynamic-naturalistic system of National Socialism, and the rationalism of Anglo-Saxon systems. Only the dynamism of National Socialism captured the spirit of a world needing a revolution. Relativism advocated adjustment to the ruling conscience. He assumed the breakdown of the bourgeois world which had supported Protestantism. He found resistance in basic Christian ethics based upon *agape.* He joined *agape* with his socialist *kairos* as a basis of a relevant Christian ethic. He expected in this chapter a more collectivist society encouraging leisure and meditation to emerge "over against a self-destructive adoration of work and activism."[19] Readers familiar with Tillich would not be startled that he argues that love cannot be defined and that he notes the chapter neglects justice. But, the neglect of the concept of power weakens the chapter. His definition of ethics concluding the book lacks the relationship to morals discussed in the first three chapters. "And this is the meaning of ethics: the expression of the ways in which love embodies itself and life is maintained and saved."[20] So it creates confusion within the manuscript.

MY SEARCH FOR ABSOLUTES

Ruth Nanda Anshen's second edited book, *My Search for Absolutes* represents Tillich's last thoughts as presented to the University of Chicago Law School and prepared for lectures at Columbia later in 1965.[21] As in the her previous book, the arguments are from the *Systematic Theology* in a more popular form and chapter three from *Christianity and the Encounter with World Religions.* She takes the

---

[19] Tillich, 92.

[20] Tillich, 95.

[21] Paul Tillich, *My Search for Absolutes, ed.* Ruth Nanda Anshen (New York: Simon and Schuster, 1967).

liberty of a twenty-two page introduction which corresponds to Tillich's thought, except for Tillich's Lutheran pessimism which cuts through her religious-humanism-optimism. The book also contains twenty-eight pages of Saul Steinberg's drawings representing Steinberg's absorption of Tillich's thought.

It is interesting that in a short book of lectures for a law school, so little is said about law though Tillich wrote and lectured on law elsewhere. Tillich's thesis is the relevance of the absolutes which qualify the relativism of knowledge, morals, and religion.

The book relates the liberal humanistic struggle against fascism and communism. Fascism has been defeated, and the struggle with Communism is engaged by liberal humanism. He fears nationalism hardening into a demonic force in the United States in the context of 1965. He seems to have forgotten the struggle with Fascism in its Nazi form, which he regarded as a struggle with Christianity in his wartime speeches into occupied Europe from 1942-44.[22] President's Eisenhower and Truman had also defined the Cold War as a Christian war against atheism. Tillich did not join in this analysis. I've regarded the struggle with Karl Marx as a struggle with his vital atheism. Tillich, of course, found Marx's deity in the sociology of revolution.

The autobiographical reflections introduce the volume. There are a few emphases which enrich his previous biographical writings. He indicates the early development of his nature mysticism and his attachment to romanticism. He clearly indicates his identity as a Lutheran Christian and that his discovery of autonomy arose in his philosophical debates with his dominating father. He credits World War I with his affirming democracy and revolution. He hints however that his social concern preceded the war and his adoption of socialism. He affirms Barth's criticism of him as fighting the Grand Inquisitor, which for Tillich is a permanent necessary fight. He

[22] Tillich, *Against the Third Reich.*

sheds no light on his Bohemian, radical lifestyle in the essay, though he has elsewhere. His writing on the dialectical yes and no to Karl Marx and Friedrich Nietzsche is clear, though it appears in many other writings.

In three brief chapters he lists his absolutes overcoming relativism: (1) the subject and object structure of the human mind; (2) the absoluteness of essences; (3) the absoluteness of the structure of being; (4) absoluteness of being itself; (5) the moral imperative; (6) justice; (7) *agape*; (8) the encounter with the Holy; and (9) the human search for ultimate reality.

Tillich's despair is best found in *The Courage to Be*, written for lectures at Yale shortly after his publication of the first volume of the *Systematic Theology*. Rollo May regards it as a response to his dissertation on anxiety which Tillich supervised. It begins with Plato's *Laches* dialogue and concludes with the despair of Heidegger, Sartre, and Nietzsche. Tillich's own affirmation of courage is made in affirming the acceptance of being itself despite the guilt, nihilism, and meaninglessness of modern society. He gives Nietzsche primary place among the existentialists and finds their work, especially in psychoanalysis, to be descriptive of modern humanity without God or meaning. He recognizes religion includes both ethics and metaphysics, but he chooses ontology to explain courage, thereby taking the term out of Plato's moral discourse into the more fundamental ontology discussed through the history of philosophy. Interpreters regard it as the most popular of his books. I find it the most difficult to read. It demands a rather detailed knowledge of the history of philosophy as well as a good deal about psychoanalytic theory, which I don't believe most of its readers possessed. It also is based in a far less optimistic world view than most Americans knew in the 1950s. To me it is his most existentialist book, which represents his own position at the time in the age he regarded as one of anxiety. Courage is not so much a moral virtue in the book as it is the key to religious understanding. Two forms of courage he lingers over are the courage to participate in the communities of one's own time which bear meaning and the courage to be one's own unique self who asserts the courage to be. Confronted by the existentialist revolt against morality, conformity, tradition, and religion, modern humanity finds life as meaningless. Even the Gods of theism are rejected, and courage is found as being itself grasps one and assures forgiveness and love. Being itself is found in the God beyond God, which appears to be like Luther's God, which absorbed non-being, despair, and meaningless into itself. Courage appears in the *Systematic Theology* within the ontological analysis but in a less portentous role than in this volume on courage. I find his life to be one of extreme courage in overcoming threatening opposition to act, and even without the ontological analysis, I find it one of his crucial virtues.

In the autobiographical remarks in *My Search for Absolutes* written in Chicago, his writing about his home at Union Theological Seminary in New York City is very affirmative. In dedicating his *Systematic Theology* to his students at the Seminary he reveals part of datedness and limited audience. The students not only heard the content as it was being thought and written, the graduate students helped him organize it. There were only a few minority students or women at the Seminary and their unique concerns are not present in the S*ystematic* or in the later writings on ethics. A *kairos* was emerging for the Black students and nearby residents of his neighborhoods at Union, Harvard, and Chicago. But somehow Tillich missed the *kairoi* of the sixties. His secretary Grace Cali wrote that he consulted students who participated in the Civil Rights struggle at Harvard,[23] but neither his written texts nor his private papers in the Harvard Archive show evidence of high participation beyond writing a Congressman about housing and giving his name to some events.

[23] Grace Cali, quoted in Mark Lewis Taylor, "Tillich's Ethics between Politics and Ontology," in *The Cambridge Companion to Paul Tillich*, ed. Russell Re Manning (Cambridge: Cambridge University Press, 2009), 190.

PERSONAL ETHICS

At the low point in her relationship with President Bill Clinton, Hillary was reported drawing on her faith by her press secretary. She remembered the counsel of her youth minister Don Jones who had read Tillich's sermon, "You Are Accepted," to her Methodist youth group. She recorded:

> Its premise is how sin and grace exist through life in constant interplay; neither is possible without the other. The mystery of grace is that you cannot look for it. Grace strikes us when we are in great pain and restlessness. Tillich wrote: "It happens or it does not happen."[24]

My experience is that Tillich often provided the words that healed the troubled. He was so aware of the healing presence of the Spirit that he listened and often provided a healing word.

The dynamics of sin and grace are, for Tillich, a meaning of human life. Sin is the separation or estrangement of the human life from itself, its neighbor, and the foundation of its being. It is the human fate to be estranged. Grace is the reunion of the self with life and itself.

Sin and grace are known by the experience of the other. I heard this theme repeated on many of Tillich's returns to preach at Union Chapel from 1960-65. I never heard the original sermon "You Are Accepted" as it was published in 1948 in the book of sermons, *The Shaking of the Foundations*.[25] The book reflected the reality of atomic bombing and the American occupation of ruined European cities. Grace overcame the chaos of separation and allows a life of "confidence and courage" which both Hillary Clinton and Paul Tillich were able to find. The despair of estrangement is a little more

---

[24] Hillary Rodman Clinton, *Living History* (New York: Simon and Schuster, 2003), 470.

[25] Paul Tillich, *The Shaking of the Foundations* (New York: Charles Scribner's Sons, 1948), 153-63.

prominent than grace in the sermon. The self-hatred with the human was better known in his generation than in others, he believed, as he had learned it from Freud and depth psychology. Social groups and nations also revealed their hatred of the other. Meaninglessness showed the alienation from the eternal.

Paul's words in Romans 7:19, "For I do not do the good I desire, but rather the evil that I do not desire" were true for Paul Tillich, who knew of the split between his true self and the estranged self. He wrote of giving in to the demonic for decades. However, grace even more bounded as provided in the light of acceptance by the ground of his being. The sermon persuades that both Paul, the apostle, and Paul, the sinner, found this light in the non-estranged picture of Jesus as the Christ. Paul confesses: "the old compulsion reigns within us as they have for decades, yet acceptance breaks through and courage and purpose are regained." The "certainty of the eternal meaning of our life" is regained. The reality of sin and grace determine life for Tillich, and he concludes: "May grace more abound within us."[26]

Tillich characteristically chose to advocate for the new in life. In a sermon following the one on acceptance he chose the Old Testament passages promising newness of life over against the cynicism of the preacher in Ecclesiastes.[27] He exults in Second Corinthians proclamation of the Christian "as new creation." He preached the sermon, "Behold I am Doing a New thing" in his sixties, and he feared our modern age was becoming old and rigid. His Europe needed a new beginning. The modern period had chosen nationalism, secularism, and scientism to control the world in its new freedoms from serfdom and ecclesiastic control. The age of enlightenment or autonomous rebellion was exhausting itself. Where was the new? It was not to be found in only a new synthesis of combining

[26] Tillich, 163.
[27] Tillich, 173-86.

aspects of the old. New things can emerge from almost any source or group. But what are the criteria to judge the important new beginnings? Moving beyond the sermon to his biography, it is possible to say for him the new had been: revolution, religious socialism, immigration into American life, the construction of his system, and then in the future, the rediscovery of interreligious dialogues with Asia. In the conclusion to the sermon he announced, "Love never ends." A new age began in the church, and it can be released from the repression which captured it.

For me, the new was released in my alliance with the new emerging from the old Black Church. This began in the 50s when I was awakened to the power of love in King's nonviolent use of the church to create freedom. It led to a life of study and action to integrate and empower Blacks in church and society and to the new energy in the "Black Lives Matter" campaign after George Floyd's murder in 2020. The release of the "new creation" for me was the finding of vocational meaning or a "calling" to which I could surrender. Tillich found it also and achieved greatness. I never could buy into a search for fulfillment which Tillich got from psychological associations. As for me it was surrender to a vocation perceived as following Christ and then being rewarded with a new life. My route is not Tillich's, but it runs parallel. I am uncertain of either road as a guide for most of my fellow Americans. We were rewarded as spiritual elites. But don't most of my fellows labor on, enduring work that is hardly a called vocation? I hear young preachers urging moral heroism upon their already determined middle-class, ageing congregations. What meaning does such moralism have? Youth ministry, which I left sixty years ago, could have more meaning than challenging middle-class America. Certainly Hillary is testimony to that reality.

Tillich's "Presidential Address" for the American Theological Society on April 14, 1944 carried forward the same arguments as

"You Are Accepted" but without basing it so directly on Saint Paul.[28] His dialectical argument was on estrangement and reconciliation in Hegel, William James, Marx, and Jung. He left only Jung and some of Erich Fromm hanging as satisfactory, and their answers were based on the essence of Christianity. Life is essentially a unity, but human existence is estranged, only by a "hidden Christology" wherein suffering in estrangement is grace realized. The state of estrangement is overcome by a unifying love. Taking his interpretation of early Hegel and early Marx together the middle-class Americans have only entertainments to explain or distract them from their estrangement. Tillich does not say so, but the pragmatism of William James combined with hope for their children would provide some purpose to overcome the estrangement. They might never find his courage to become the unique self. But their courage to volunteer and participate in the groups of their common life went a long way towards overcoming meaninglessness. The poor of America have a much harder time as they scramble to provide food, housing, and education. They correspond closer to the lumpen-proletarians of Marx, who are lost. Meanwhile, America provides some welfare and entertainment to assuage the loss of meaning for the estranged. Also of note is that the Christian symbolism often lives with the William James' religiosity to provide meaning to those who have not the basic needs of life.

Tillich's anti-moralism is so strong that it is not expected of him to provide a list of moral duties. He clarifies his goals for an optimum life in a dialogue with Carl Rogers in 1965 in San Diego.[29] The two found themselves in general agreement. Rogers was pleased, as a therapist, if the client attained a "greater openness to experience." The goal would be for one to become aware of self and

---

[28] Paul Tillich, "Estrangement and Reconciliation," in *The Meaning of Health*, ed. Perry LeFevre (Chicago: Exploration Press, 1984): 1-15.

[29] "Paul Tillich and Carl Rogers: A Dialogue," in *The Meaning of Health*, 202.

more realistically perceptive the world. He hoped for a client to be in process of becoming more oneself and becoming realistic about his self-processes and about his place in the world. This realization would lead one to become more social and move towards good citizenship. Tillich agreed with the openness and affirmed the need to be open to symbols which could lead to an experience of God. Tillich affirmed the need for a social relationship as part of the larger realization of *agape* or listening love. Finding ultimate meaning in life was by way of faith and love. Decisions for action arose, he argued, out of the situation and not out of any philosophy of values. Rogers in the dialogue kept the discussion at a humanist level whereas Tillich would move the conversation towards ultimate questions or religion. For Tillich, a fulfilled personal morality would be to live responsibly in a vocation for human good, to be guided by listening love of the whole situation, to live responsibly within one's destiny in maximum freedom, and given estrangement from the divine, to love God.

HANNAH'S ANGER

Eight years after Paul's death, Hannah published her version of their married life.[30] The "Open marriage" of their earliest years in Germany had not worked for her in America. Tillich had taken too many lovers, and her extramarital affairs, heterosexual and homosexual, had not compensated. Her book combines fantasy from her earlier unpublished erotic novels and from her attempts at play writing. I found it to be a very erotic work in itself even without regard to the historical characters. Hannah, as a non-Christian Freudian, had a rich imagination of eroticism, according to her psychologist son, Rene. He wrote frankly that regarding Paul's sex life her book was not to be trusted. Fred Parrella, the longtime Secretary of the North American Paul Tillich Society told me that she admitted she

[30] Hannah Tillich, *From Time.*

wrote it for money and that she was sorry she published the book. I find the book to be a work based on fearful imagination written out of anger by a very hurt woman. I accept as fact that Paul Tillich had many extramarital affairs and that he appreciated pornography. He failed to give his wife the *agape* she sought and deserved. Though Hannah and I talked a couple of times, I never discussed the book with her. She was very fond of my book, *Paul Tillich's Radical Social Thought*.[31] Discussions with their daughter, Mutie, about the book and sexuality produced agreement. It did not need to be written except for Hannah's voice to be expressed. Not everyone agrees with me, but I find that it hurt Tillich's reputation badly, and it is harder to get a hearing for the beauty of his life's work.

I found Rollo May's book, which Hannah urged him to write, to be a more helpful guide to personal matters regarding Paul Tillich than her own. His psychotherapy background allowed him to explore issues in Tillich's life more profoundly.[32] He introduces Paul's reaction to his mother's early death as evoking his longing for the feminine and as a search for her replacement. I think he is correct in emphasizing the Bohemian nature of their lifestyle in the Weimar Republic. He notes the war shattering Tillich's conventional morality, though I would emphasize that more than May does. His suffering from post-traumatic stress disorder, their divorces to marry each other, and their wild lifestyle created conflicts not easily resolvable under the best of circumstances. They continued the original Bohemian "Open marriage" in New York, and it failed to provide the nourishment Hannah needed. Her ambitions to write were not fulfilled, and as the younger woman she could not compete with the one who was so loved by crowds, writers, intellectuals, and other women. He knew he hurt her, and she reminded him often with her anger. His conscience led him to harbor unresolved guilt, and the

[31] Ronald Stone, *Paul Tillich's Radical Social Thought* (Atlanta: John Knox Press, 1980).

[32] Rollo May, *Paulus* (New York: Harper & Row Publishers, 1973).

guilt soured the relationship until it was almost unbearable. When trust is lost and guilt left unresolved there is not much to hold a marriage together. They discussed divorce and came close, but professional considerations held them back from their second divorce, and Tillich, according to his son, rejected divorce and the man leaving his wife for another woman. Critics of Tillich's erotic life should read Rollo May and Rene Tillich's analyses before commenting too knowingly on the life of Tillich.[33]

Tillich questioned his own erotic life as to whether his way of erotic life was a creative venture or a failure. I think "failure," as he seemed to imply, is the better choice. Others like Rollo May find it creative. Hannah deserved better as a wife. She apparently was very difficult to live with, as her son Rene witnessed. They both lived with a great deal of marital pain. His writings on morals pretty consistently reject strict sexual ethics and pronounce particularly harshly on the American tradition influenced by Puritanism. But he couldn't free his own conscience from censure. His declaration of a sensitive conscience necessarily being a guilty one is an exaggeration, but it was his own.

Perhaps the best response by theologians is represented by Mary Ann Stenger and Rachel Baard who, I think, admit the revelations of Hannah cause pain among women and require them to take his thought selectively and critically.[34] The context of the dispute is the 1930s through 1965, a time of moral relaxation among first, the Germans, and then the Americans regarding sexual freedom.

---

[33] Rene Tillich, "My Father, Paul Tillich" in Tillich-Studien, Band 5. "Spurensuche: Lebens-und Denkwege Paul Tillichs" (Ilona Nord, Yorick Spiegel, 1998).

[34] Mary Ann Stenger, "Thought and Life: The Cases of Heidegger and Tillich, Response to Owen Thomas," Papers from the Annual Meeting of North America Paul Tillich Society (November 1964): 29-45; Rachel Baard, "Tillich and Feminism," in *The Cambridge Companion to Paul Tillich*, ed. Russel Re Manning (Cambridge: Cambridge University Press, 2009): 273-87.

Among my panoply of American heroes of the 1960s I include John F. Kennedy, Robert Kennedy, and Martin Luther. King, Jr.; they are best appreciated for social-political actions and not as model husbands. I love Reinhold Niebuhr more, and he could serve as a model of a husband, but he responded to the exposure of Tillich's adultery at Harvard as saying he was glad it was not revealed at Union Theological Seminary.

Regarding ethical theory, Tillich's romanticism did not serve him well. His lovable personality charmed most, and many invited intimacy which he could have bypassed. The romanticism was probably overly critical of moral discipline and left him disappointed. He was also critical of his earlier political utopianism; he needed to stay closer to his "faithful realism."

Tendencies toward situationalism, betrayed him. He tried to hold moral principles, and even traditional moral teachings like the Ten Commandments, in high respect, but in his personal life he needed more discipline to live out his *agape* for his wife. It seems to me that his definition of *agape* as the drive for reunion is not the most adequate. Jesus portrayed *agape* as the love for neighbor. The Good Samaritan did not need union with the mugged stranger on the road to Jericho; he needed to provide for the neighbor's needs. *Agape* is the summary and highest principle of Christian morality, and it does not need to be subsumed under mysticism or ontology. Tillich's Augustinian-Lutheran-existentialist anthropology found religious meaning in faith, acceptance, and forgiveness and not in perfect moral behavior. Unfortunately, the discussion of his morals related to practice were focused in the North American Paul Tillich Society under the motif of comparing Heidegger's political morality and Tillich's sexual morality. If they were to be used, a more helpful discussion would have discussed them both in the same dimension.[35]

On the other hand, I know of no other theologian-philosopher who so fulfilled his calling or completed his vocation more. No life can meet every potential; he could have experienced life south of the equator or condemned the war in Vietnam more sharply. He contributed to women's liberation, but he could have done more given his commitments in 1918 to women leadership in the church. He moved against racism, but given the University of Chicago context in the 1960s, he could have been bolder. Still, at the end he was engaged with Buddhism and speaking around the country on a variety of theological-political topics as requested. His bold theological-moral denunciations of Senators McCarthy and Goldwater revealed his political courage and passion. The power, courage, and fulfillment of the *power* of his *agape* is seen in the corpus of his work.

TILLICH'S ETHICAL THEMES

Chapter one introduces ethics as the study of morals. In the beginning he is following Kant in affirming the Unconditional or Absoluteness of the moral imperative. He also understood the relational quality of the application of any norm. He affirmed autonomy but is passionate concerning moving to a free society of theonomy governed by justice.

Chapter two is the narrative of his finding community in socialist-religious circles and in intimate circles of discussion among friends. His three socialist circles: the Kairos Circle, the Frankfurt School, and the Fellowship of Socialist Christians encouraged his critique of capitalism, provided community, and advocated justice and hope for transformation in critical reception of Marxism. The theme of the necessity of community is continued in *Love, Power,*

[35] Owen Thomas, "Thought and Life: The Cases of Heidegger and Tillich;" Julia A. Lamm, "A Hermeneutics of Revulsion: Response to Owen C. Thomas," both in Papers from the Annual Meeting of North America Paul Tillich Society (November 1964): 29-45.

and Justice and particularly in *Systematic Theology*, vol. 3, and his late ethical writings.

Chapter three provides the story of "Paulus among the Jews." From his defense of Jewish students at Frankfurt to his longtime chairmanship of Self-Help for Emigres from Central Europe he demonstrated love through action for Jewish neighbors. The defense of Judaism was a moral imperative which he carried out practically and theoretically. Believing the defense of Jews was an imperative which should be taught in churches, he worked to remove anti-Jewish materials from Sunday school materials and began his wartime public speeches to Europe condemning anti-Semitism.

Chapter four correlates Marxist morals with Protestant morals. Despite the awkwardness of their union, Marxism for him is a major corrective of Christian social ethics as practiced in Germany and the United States. From his 1918 rally speech, to the Independent Socialists in Berlin, to his 1963 *Systematic Theology,* he continued his "Yes" and "no" utilization of Marx. I personally continued the dialogue in Berlin, Prague, and Budapest during the Cold War, and in visits to Russia.

Chapter five narrates five instances of Tillich's defining the goals in World War II for the allies. The articulation of the purpose of the war meets the just war theory's necessity for a just cause. Later arguments by Tillich also absorb other principles of the theory: proportionality and just outcomes. He argued that nuclear war could not meet the just-war criteria.

Chapter six shows Tillich's commitments to ecumenical church work and his hopes for keeping it faithful and realistic. The high-class optimism of John Foster Dulles drove the Commission's work for the Federal Council of Churches during World War II. Tillich wanted it to be more realistic and to realize the need for economic security beyond capitalism. He supported the church-movement for the United Nations, but he knew the anarchy of the world's nations in a revolutionary situation would thwart the Commission on a Just and Durable Peace from achieving its utopian dreams. He hoped for a better world than the clash of capitalism and communism promised. Germany needed to be rebuilt with a European Federation that could control it. Dulles, an establishment Presbyterian, dreamed of a capitalist world order governing through the United Nations. Tillich, as a Lutheran German-socialist émigré, thought he destroyed the presumption of Dulles' utopia.

Chapter seven develops Tillich's understanding of power and his conviction that power considerations are necessary for ethics. It relates power to justice and love in Tillich's ontology. So these three concepts provide the framework for his ethics of war, peace, and economics. Placing the discussion of the concepts from the German Empire in the context of the American Empire grounds Tillich's ethics squarely in the context of Faithful Realism.

Chapter eight compared and contrasted religious socialist ideas to those of Latin American liberation theology. It detailed the emergence of justice as Tillich's primary, but historically unfulfilled, social concept. Tillich used liberation as a goal for World War II and hoped for European social security for the masses there in religious socialism and democracy. Gutiérrez hoped for socialism for Latin America and liberation through revolution. Neither saw their dreams fulfilled, as the mixed economies of Europe became more secular and the security states and the Vatican suppressed liberation in Latin America. Justice as a primary and necessary term for Tillich's ethics is clarified in the comparison. I believe more regulation of the corporations, larger state-supplied opportunities for the masses, and greater equality through taxation are all historical projects for the Christian ethicist today in the United States, given its history and distribution of power. The above mixed economy-welfare economics is a realistic tilted reading of Tillich now a half-century past his death. The religious quality of his hoped for theonomous society is far from realization, given the conservatism of Christians in the US. But it remains a personal option and many of our political leaders on the left represent it.

Chapter nine examines the term *kairos*, which Tillich used regularly in social analysis. Its revolutionary, transformative perspective is analyzed through eight theological-reflection movements for social change. Care is needed to ground the term in faithful realism rather than romanticism.

Chapter ten tells the story of Tillich and his friends reacting to the transformation of international politics by nuclear power and policies. Reinhold Niebuhr, John Bennett, and ecumenical Christianity join Tillich in opposing the use of nuclear weapons. Tillich goes further than the others in calling for creative resistance to the weapons. All three agree, contrary to US policy, to no first use of nuclear weapons. That resistance still remains on the agenda of Christian ethics. Tillich was seriously criticized for applying just war criteria to the defense of Berlin and rejecting the use of such weapons for his home city.

Chapter eleven regards the dialogue with other religions and quasi-religions to be of the essence of the search for a meaningful peace. It is a moral obligation. Presupposing and having fulfilled a dialogue with Judaism, late in life, Tillich undertook his dialogue with Zen Buddhism mostly within the Kyoto School. Several of the dialogues were recorded. Fundamental disagreements were discussed and the need for further discussion noted. The engaged Buddhism of Vietnam has overcome the lack of social-historical vigor noted by Paul Tillich and accepted by some of the Zen masters. They were gentle in their needed critique of the aggressiveness of Christianity in Asia. The dialogue requirement was fulfilled more by Tillich than by most Western theologians.

The final chapter, twelve, returns to the major theme of *agape* for his ethics and emphasizes the discovery of the limits of morality in the person to person encounter. The final sources of his late ethics all confirm the threefold pattern discussed in the first chapter on ethics and morals and adds love as the motivation for moral action.

Agape is the formal absolute, the summary of moral wisdom, the careful listening to the moral situation, and the motivation for the moral life.

The twelve themes represent a complete ethic or theory of morals for the modern person. They present a more complicated ethic than most people will follow. For those who seek an ethic grounded in the depths of a religious ethic combined with principles they are a very live option. His life combines wisdom and courage. His particular context in the Bohemian life of Weimar after the trenches of World War I and the nuclear crisis and the Cold War led him, I believe, to his faithful realism adequate for guiding the politics of his new home in America even if his socialism was too utopian for American politics. The experimentation in sexual morality was too influenced by romanticism and situationalism and left him personally guilty. However, the psychological pain he suffered was caused as much by the world situation he engaged as it was of personal grief. His work in the full development of the twelve themes was an ethic of a fulfilled life which few can emulate.

ACKNOWLEDGMENTS

I want to acknowledge my debt to John Stumme, who as a student in a political philosophy tutorial at Union Theological Seminary persuaded me that on some issues around Karl Marx and religion Paul Tillich was wiser than Reinhold Niebuhr. So in the 1970s my pursuit of Paul Tillich began. James Luther Adams, the dean of Tillich scholars, warmly welcomed me to the Tillich Archives at the Harvard University Divinity School Library. He shared his knowledge and expertise very readily. Often, soon after I arrived as the Library opened in the morning, James would show up to share something he had remembered during the night. My colleague Walter Wiest, a doctoral student of Tillich's, supported my efforts in Tillich scholarship, and we combined *Love, Power, and Justice* with the new books on Black power as we planned our first course on ethics on the picket line to integrate the Construction-industry guilds in Pittsburgh, 1969. My late friend Erdmutie Tillich Farris provided many insights into her father's soul to me, and I thank her for her assistance.

I've added previous publications to my current thought to build this book on ethics. Some of the argument from *The Socialist Decision*, Tillich's major philosophy of politics book, was repeated in different topical chapters because of its central importance to his thought. All previous publications have been altered or reedited for this volume. Chapter two was published in Mary Ann Stenger and Ronald H. Stone, *Dialogues of Paul Tillich* (Macon: Mercer University Press, 2002): 164-87. Chapter three was published originally in the *North American Paul Tillich Society Newsletter* 20, no. 2 (April 1994): 2-8. Chapter four was published in Mary Ann Stenger and

Ronald H. Stone, *Dialogues of Paul Tillich* (Macon: Mercer University Press, 2002): 150-63. Chapter five was published in Mary Ann Stenger and Ronald H. Stone, *Dialogues of Paul Tillich* (Macon: Mercer University Press, 2002): 222-40. Chapter six was published in the *International Yearbook for Tillich Research: Brokenness and Reconciliation*, vol. 14, eds. Bryan Wagoner et al. (Berlin: De Gruyter, 2020): 203-14. Chapter seven was published in *International Yearbook for Tillich Research*, vol. 9, eds. Christian Danz, Marc Dumas, Werner Schüßler, Mary Ann Stenger, and Erdmann Sturm (Berlin: De Gruyter, 2014): 47-62. Chapter eight was originally published in *Laval theologique et philosophique* 44, no. 2 (June 1988): 155-67. Chapter nine is published simultaneously in Thomas Bandy, eds., *Why Tillich? Why Now?* (Macon: Mercer University Press, 2021). Chapter ten was originally in a different form in Mary Ann Stenger and Ronald H. Stone, *Dialogues of Paul Tillich* (Macon: Mercer University Press, 2002): 241-53.

My son Professor Randall Stone assisted in technological production of this volume, and my wife Linda Haddad proofread the manuscript with me, and I wish to thank them both with my love. I recognize and thank Director Marc Jolley of Mercer University Press and the staff Marsha Luttrell and Mary Beth Kosowski for their kindness and efficient work in bringing this volume to publication.

BIBLIOGRAPHY

Tillich, Paul. Das *System der Wissenschaft nach Gegenstanden und Methoden: Ein Enwurf.* Gottingen Vanderhoaeck & Ruprecht, 1923. Translated by Paul Wiebe. *The System of the Sciences according to Objects and Methods.* Lewisburgh, PA: Bucknell University Press, 1981.

________. Die religiose Lage *der Gegenwart.* Berlin. Ullstein, 1926. *The Religious Situation.* Translated by H. Richard Niebuhr, New York: Henry Holt and Co., 1932.

________. *The Interpretation of History.* New York: Charles Scribner's sons, 1936.

________. "The Gospel and the State." *Crozer Quarterly* 15/4 (1938): 241-61.

________. "The Religious Symbol." *Journal of Liberal Religion* 2 (Summer, 1940) 13-33.

________. "War Aims." *Protestant Digest.* New York, 1941.

________. "Protestant Principles." *The Protestant 4/5* (April-May *1942):* 17.

________. "Man and Society in Religious Socialism." *Christianity and Society 8/4 (1943)*: 10-20.

________. et. al. *The Christian Answer.* Edited by Henry Pitney P. Van Dusen. New York: Charles Scribner's Sons, 1945.

________. "The Two types of Philosophy of Religion." *Union Seminary Quarterly Review* 1 (May, 1946): 3:13.

________. *The Protestant Era.* Translated by James Luther Adams. Chicago: University of Chicago Press, 1948.

________. "Beyond Religious Socialism." *Christian Century* 66 (15 June 1949): 732-33.

________. *Systematic Theology.* Three Volumes. Chicago: University of Chicago Press, 1951-1963.

________. *The Courage to Be.* New Haven: Yale University Press, 1952

________. *Love, Power, and Justice.* New York/London: Oxford University Press, 1954

________. *Biblical Religion and the Search for Ultimate Reality.* Chicago: University of Chicago Press, 1955.

________. *Dynamics of Faith.* New York: Harper & Row, 1957.

________. *Theology of Culture.* Edited by Robert Kimball. London: Oxford University Press, 1959.

________. "The Christian and Marxist View of Man." Second Edition. Harvard Archive: Universal Christian Council for Life and Work, 1959.

________. "Sin and Grace in the Theology of Reinhold Niebuhr." in *Reinhold Niebuhr: A Prophetic Voice in Our Time,* Edited by Harold Landon, Greenwich: Seabury Press, 27-41.

________. *Christianity and the Encounter of World Religions.* New York: Columbia University Press, 1963.

________. *Morality and Beyond.* New York: Harper & Row, 1963. Republished, Edited by William Schweiker, Louisville: Westminster John Knox Press, 1995.

________. *Ultimate Concern Tillich in Dialogue.* Edited by D. Mackensie Brown. New York: Harper & Row, 1965.

________. "Rejoinder." in *The Journal of Religion.* 46 (January 1966): 190.

________. *My Search for Absolutes,* Edited by Ruth Nanda Anshen. New York: Simon and Schuster, 1967.

________. *A History of Christian Thought,* Edited by Carl E. Braaten. New York: Harper & Row, 1969.

________. *My Travel Diary: 1936.* New York: Harper & Row, 1970.

________. *Political Expectation,* Edited by James Luther Adams. New York: Harper & Row, 1971.

________. *The Socialist Decision,* Translated by Franklin Sherman. New York: Harper & Row, 1977.

________. *The Meaning of Health,* Edited by Perry LeFevre. Chicago: Exploration Press, 1984.

________. *The Theology of Peace*, Edited by Ronald H. Stone. Louisville: Westminster/John Knox Press, 1990.

________. "A Dialogue between Paul Tillich and Hisamatsu Shin'ichi." in *The Encounter of Religions and Quasi-Religions,* Edited by Terrence Thomas. Lewiston: Edwin Mellen Press, 1990. 75-170.

________. *Against the Third Reich: Paul Tillich's War time Radio Broadcasts into Nazi Germany,* Edited by Ronald H. Stone and Matthew Lon Weaver; Translated by Matthew Lon Weaver. Louisville: Westminster John Knox Press, 1998.

SECONDARY BIBLIOGRAPHY

Adams, James Luther. *Paul Tillich's Philosophy of Culture, Science, and Religion.* New York: Schocken Books, 1995.

Adams, James Luther, Wilhelm Pauck, and Roger L. Shinn, Editors. *The Theology of Paul Tillich.* San Francisco: Harper & Row, 1985.

Alves, Rubem A. *Protestantism and Repression: A Brazilian Case Study.* Maryknoll: Orbis Books, 1985.

Amelung, Edward. "Religious Socialism as an Ideology: A Study of the Kairos Circle in Germany between 1919 and 1933." Ph.D. dissertation, Harvard University, 1962.

Batchelder, Robert C. *The Irreversible Decision 1939-1950.* Boston: Houghton Mifflin Co., 1961.

Bennett, John C., editor. *Nuclear Weapons and the Conflict of Conscience. New York: Scribner, 1962.*

Brown, Robert McAffee. *Gustavo Gurierrrez.* Atlanta: John Knox Press, 1980.

Brown, Robert McAffee, Editor. *Kairos Three Prophetic Challenges to the Church.* Grand Rapids: Wm. B. Eerdmans ,1990.

Carey, John J. Editor. *Tillich Studies: 1975.* Tallahassee: North American Paul Tillich Society, 1975.

________. Editor. *Kairos and Logos.* Cambridge: North American Paul Tillich Society, 1978.

________. Editor. *Theonomy and Autonomy.* Macon: Mercer University Press, 1984.

________. Editor. *Being and Doing: Paul Tillich as Ethicist.* Macon: Mercer University Press, 1987.

Cooper, Terry D. *Paul Tillich and Psychology.* Macon: Mercer University Press, 2006.

Dulles, John Foster. "The American Churches in time of War" in *Federal Council* Bulletin XXIV (January, 1941) 6.

Garcia, Ismael. *Justice in Latin American Theology of Liberation.* Atlanta: John Knox Press, 1987.

Graves-Fitzsimmons, Guthrie. "Igniting a Moral Revival" in *Union's Collective.* New York: Union theological Seminary (2018) 8-13.

Fishman, Hertzel. *American Protestantism and a Jewish State.* Detroit: Wayne State University Press, 75.

Gay, Peter. "Weimar Culture: the Outsider as Insider." in *Perspectives in American History* 2 (1968).

Gutierrez, Gustavo. *We Drink from Our Own Wells: The Spiritual Journey of a People.* Maryknoll: Orbis Press, 1983.

________. *On Job.* Maryknoll: Orbis Press, 1984.

________. *A Theology of Liberation:* Maryknoll: Orbis Books, 1998.

Hammond, Guyton. *Man in Estrangement: A Comparison of the Thought of Paul Tillich and Erich Fromm.* Nashville: Vanderbilt University Press, 1965.

________.Review of Ronald H. Stone*: Reinhold Niebuhr and Paul Tillich at Union Seminary in New York.* In Bulletin of the North American Paul Tillich Society, XXXIX/ 2 (Spring 2013) 3-5.

Halpern, Ben. "Zionism." In *International Encyclopedia of the Social Sciences.* New York: The Macmillan Co. (1968) 593.

Handy, Robert T. "Christian Action in Perspective" in *Christianity and Society*

21 (Summer 1956) 10-4.
Heimann, Eduard. *Kapitlismus und Sozilizmus.* Potsdam: Alfred Protte, 1931.
Horkheimer, Max. *Werk und Wirken Paul Tillichs.* Stuttgart: Evangelisches Verlagswerk, 1967.
Jay, Martin. *The Dialectical Imagination: A History of the Frankfurt School and the Institute of Social Research, 1923-1950.* Boston: Little, Brown, and Company, 1973.
May, Rollo. *Paulus.* New York: Harper & Row, 1973.
Lebacqz, Karen, *Six Theories of Justice.* Minneapolis: Augsburg Publishing House, 1986.
Niebuhr, Reinhold. Review of Tillich's *The Religious Situation. The World Tomorrow* 15/23 (21 December 1932) 41-2.
________. Review of Tillich's *Interpretation of History. Radical Religion* (winter 1936) 21-2.
________. "The *Contribution* of Paul Tillich." *Religion in Life* 6/4 (Autumn 1937) 574-81.
________. "Jews after the War." *The Nation (*21 February 1942*)* 214-16, 253-55.
________. 'The Atomic Issue." *Christianity and Crisis* 5/17 (15 October) 7.
________."The Hydrogen Bomb." *Christianity and Society* (Spring, 1950) 5-7.
________. Review of *Biblical Religion and the Search for Ultimate Reality. Union Seminary Quarterly Review* 11/2 (January 1956) 59-60.
________. *Pious and Secular America.* New York: Charles Scribner's Sons, 1958.
________. "Biblical Thought and Ontological Speculation in Tillich's Theology." In *The Theology of Paul Tillich,* edited by Charles W. Kegley and Robert w. Bretall. New York: Macmillan, 1961. 216-17.
________. *Man's Nature and His Communities.* New York: Charles Scribner's Sons, 1956.
Pasewark, Kyle A. *A Theology of Power.* Minneapolis: Augsburg Fortress, 1993.
Pauck, Wilhelm and Marion Pauck. *Paul Tillich: His Life and Thought.* San Francisco: Harper & Row, 1976.
Shinn, roger, L. "Tension and Unity in the Ethics of Paul Tillich: An Exploration." In John J. Carey, *Beng and Doing.* Macon: Mercer University Press, (1987) 9-28.
Stenger, Mary Ann and Ronald H. Stone. *The Dialogues of Paul Tillich.* Macon: Mercer University Press, 2002.
Sone, Ronald H. *Paul Tillich's Radical Social Thought.* Atlanta: John Knox Press, 1980.
________. "The Zionism of Paul Tillich and Reinhold Niebuhr," In *Tantur Yearbook 1980-81.* Jerusalem: Tantur (1981) 219-33.
________. *The Ultimate Imperative.* Cleveland: The Pilgrim Press, 1999.

________. *Politics and Faith: Reinhold Niebuhr and Paul Tillich at Union Seminary in New York.* Macon: Mercer University Press, 2012.

Stumme, John R. *Socialism in Theological Perspective: A Study of Paul Tillich, 1918-1933.* Missoula: Scholars Press, 1978.

Taylor, Mark Lewis. "Tillich's Ethics: between Politics and Ontology." In Russell Re Manning, Editor, *The Cambridge Companion to Paul Tillich.* Cambridge: Cambridge University Press, 2008. 189-207.

Tillich, Hannah, *From Time to Time.* New York: Stein and Day, 1973.

Tillich, Rene. "My Father, Paul Tillich' in Tillich-Studien, Band 5. "Spurensuche: Lebens-und Denkwege Paul Tillichs." Illona Nord: Yorikc Spiegel, 1998.

Wagoner, Bryan L. *Prophetic Interruptions.* Macon: Mercer University Press, 2017.

Ward, W. R. *Theology, Sociology and Politics: The German Protestant Social Conscience 1890-1933.* Berne: Peter Lang Publishers, 1979.

Weaver, Matthew Lon. *Religious Internationalism: War and Peace in the Thought of Paul Tillich.* Macon: Mercer University Press, 2010.

Yip, Francis Ching-Wah. *Capitalism as Religion.* Cambridge: Harvard University Press, 2010.

INDEX